Barefoot Zone

Walking the Spiritual Path

Sally Howell Johnson

Kirk House Publishers
Minneapolis, Minnesota

Barefoot Zone
Walking the Spiritual Path

Sally Howell Johnson

ISBN – 10: 1-933794-36-4
ISBN – 13: 978-1-933794-36-5

Library of Congress Control Number: 2010941467

Kirk House Publishers, PO Box 390750, Minneapolis, MN 55439
www.kirkhouse.com
Manufactured in the United Sates of America

Dedication

To my Mom, who gave me the love of words . . .

Table of Contents

Preface

Spiritual and spirituality are words that have been appropriated by many diffeent groups and organizations. I recently had a manuscript submitted with the subtitle, "Business Spirituality." It had nothing to do with a life lived in the presence of a living God.

For many, spirituality is a quest, a search for an inner peace. That quest is often a solitary activity because the goal is achived as the activities of the world are shut out.

For others spirituality is found in a "mountain top" experience, where, usually in the company of others, one reaches a feeling of oneness with fellow humans and with God.The mountain top is called the mountain top because we always come back down to another reality.

One definition of spirituality is that it is a demeanor, a life outlook that comes from a life consciously lived in the presence of God.

As you will see from Sally Howell Johnson's account of her spiritual journey, she is aware of herself being in the presence of a living, loving God both in the solitude of a quiet place and on the freeway amidst speeding, agressive automobiles. God is everywhere in her world, and her awareness of God's presence reveals her spirituality.

As you walk with Sally on her spiritual path, may you increasingly be aware of the continuing and continous presence of God.

Take off your shoes, with her enter the Barefoot Zone.

—The Publisher

Introduction

Moses was keeping the flock of his father-in-law Jethro, the priest of Midian; he led his flock beyond the wilderness, and came to Horeb, the mountain of God. There the angel of God appeared to him in a flame of fire out of a bush; he looked, and the bush was blazing, yet it was not consumed. Then Moses said, "I must turn aside and look at this great sight, and see why the bush is not burned up." When God saw that he had turned aside, God called to him out of the bush, "Moses, Moses!" And he said, "Here I am." Then God spoke, "Come no closer! Remove the sandals from your feet, for the place on which you are standing is holy ground."   —Exodus 3:1-5

For as long as I can remember, this story from Exodus has been my favorite scripture. Though the story of our human walk with God may initially be outlined in the book of Genesis, for me, our response to God and our walk on this amazing earth begins in these opening verses in Exodus. This account of Moses' experience with the flaring forth of God always brings me joy and reminds me to keep awake to God's presence in the midst of the every day. This rare conversation between the Holy One and a human being challenges me to be open to the many sacred surprises that make up my daily walk. Who knows when I might be awakened to the sound of God's voice from a blazing bush, in the song of a bird, or through the gift of a sunset which might cause me, like Moses, to have courage enough to say "Here I am!"?

More than three years ago I began a daily blog I simply called "Pause." My reflections were posted most mornings on the website of Hennepin Avenue United Methodist Church where I have been in ministry for nearly twenty-five years. When I began these writings, they were simply meant to be a "pause" for others to bring a time of spiritual reflection to an ordinary day. As I continued, they became a daily practice for me of prayer, meditation, and being awake to the burning bushes that appear on my path. "Pause" began as an opportunity for those in our community to check in with a spiritual thought from their church, but over time people from around the country and the world have communicated with me about those writings. This has been a great gift to me—connecting with people I will never know, but who have found something helpful in this break from their regular routine.

In one of the early blog posts, I wrote:

Outside our kitchen window stands a winged euonymous bush. In the fall months, it is so bold in its bright reddish orange leaves that it is clear where it gets its popular name: burning bush." I found myself distracted over and over by its brilliance, drawn to its autumn beauty. In my distraction I was comforted by thinking about what poet Mary Oliver might say: "What else should I have been doing?!"

Later as I walked past the bush. . . .yet another stop to take in its glory. . . I got in my car and headed out to some appointments. One stop was at a friend's new yoga studio. As I walked into the entry way, I was greeted by a lovely framed sign: Barefoot Zone. On each side of the entry, shelves stood with shoes of various sizes and styles, obediently placed there before heading into "the zone." Those who walked into the studio did not bring any grit or grime from the outside into the space, only the sure, smooth print of their glorious feet. Grounded soles, nothing separated their flesh from the finely grained wood of the floor.

I thought about these two seemingly disconnected experiences— burning bush, barefoot zone. I thought about God's words to Moses: "Take off your sandals; you are standing on holy ground." Whether it is the firey red of the winged euonymous or the still green grass of the waning days of fall, every day we are invited by the presence of the Holy One blazing forth before our very eyes, to stand on holy ground. Every day we are welcomed to the Barefoot Zone.

If you are out and about today and see a woman walking happily along, without her shoes, that most likely will be me. I am headed into the Barefoot Zone. . . . Join me?

Writing "Pause" every day has given me the opportunity to be awake to the Spirit's movement in my daily walk, to be open to the burning bushes, and to take the time to honor those moments through words. I often say that I believe one of the primary responsibilities of being human is to give voice to the awe and wonder with which we are confronted daily. This becomes our response to the gift of this glorious creation in which we come to know the fuller face of God. We are the ones with words. We are the psalmists. This is the work we are called to do.

Moses' burning bush experience was the beginning of a very long journey, one he really did not want to take. After his "Here I am," he embarked on a journey filled with challenges, opportunities, mountain top triumphs, as well as tedious, tiring, and boring days. His companions adored him when things were going well and whined and complained when they were disappointed or inconvenienced. Sound familiar?

Each of us is called to the amazing journey called life. Many of us seek to discover how we walk this path surrounded by the Mystery. The Buddhist monk, Thich Nhat Hahn, says: "We all have an appointment with life and the time is now." The following reflections are an invitation to notice your path, to watch for the burning bushes, and to remove your shoes. This holy ground we trod is the Barefoot Zone.

PART ONE

Walking Gently on the Earth

In the beginning God created . . . earth, water, sky, creatures that swim, crawl, and fly, those on four legs, and those on two, sun, moon, stars, planets, all that grows upon the earth for beauty and for food. And it was good. Very, very good. This is the first story of our sacred texts. It is told in different ways, with varying emphases, depending on where humans are located around the world. It is the primary story of our beginning, our genesis. It is a story that teaches us of the ever creative Source from which we spring.

Embracing how the Holy One is known in creation has been a gift in my life. From the beauty of the southern Ohio hills of my childhood to the power and majesty of the lakes and woods of Minnesota, I have been blessed to be awake to God's presence in these lands I have called home. The presence of trees have sustained me and helped me to know the God who is grounded and strong. The song of birds has lifted my spirits and surrounded me with the vulnerability of the One who is love. The rivers I cross daily—the mighty Mississippi and the circuitous Minnesota— allow me to honor the many tributaries that feed and nurture my life. The wisdom of the seasons always remind me of the sacred cycles of birth, life, death, and resurrection, of which we are all a part.

The following reflections were written after I had the good fortune to be awake to how the Holy showed up for me in this amazing and beautiful creation. From winter to spring, from summer to fall, it is, indeed, very, very good.

The whole earth is a living icon of the face of God.

St. John Damascene

Mountains

Recently I sat on a plane that flew so close to the top of Mt. Rainier that it felt as if I could reach out and touch it. The sun was shining off the snow that makes its home on the peaks. The sky was so clear and blue it seemed as if we were all suspended in an amazing piece of art—which, of course, we were. It was one of those moments in which you have the intense realization that you are a part of something very large, something full of beauty, something beyond comprehension . . . something sacred.

As my son and I looked out the window at this amazing sight, I turned to him with a glint of tears in my eyes and said, "That's something that can get inside of you and not let go." He knew what I meant and gave me a smile and a squeeze. It will now be his privilege, when the clouds lift in Seattle, to see mountains with regularity as he begins college in this amazing city, this beautiful landscape. In addition to the lakes and water that have shaped him, he will now have the opportunity to be held and changed by the peaks and summits of mountains.

Each of us carries with us the landscape to which we were born. The trees and plants we knew as children travel someplace just below the surface of our skin. The DNA passed on to us by our ancestors is mixed with the soil, water, air, and scenery they called home. As we grow and travel to other places, we either find home in the soil and sights we experience, or we know they are not the place for us and we move on. And believe I have met people who are still searching for that place.

It is my hope, my prayer, that our son learns to look out at the power and beauty of the mountains that now surround him and find an extension of some place already deep within: A place that brings peace and stability. A place that helps him hone further the person he is becoming. A place of calm and a new way of defining home. While I always want him to have the lakes and prairies, the city and view of the Mississippi flowing through his veins, I also want him to find the awe and mystery of what it means to look into the distance and see that he is surrounded by these summits that are ancient, strong, larger than life itself.

The scriptures are filled with references to mountains. The psalms, in particular, sing the praises for how the Holy is known by those in the presence of mountains: "Your righteousness is like the mighty mountains"(Psalm 36). "On the holy mountain stands the city God created"(Psalm 87). The ancients also believed God lived on the mountain: "In days to come the mountain of God's house shall be established as the highest of the mountains, shall be raised above the hills"(Isaiah 2:2).

I am more of the mind and heart that God lives in all places. It is when we develop our sacred eyes to see that Presence that we have the encounter that brings us to the place we will call home. And so today, with my feet firmly planted on Minnesota soil, I look out my window and see the last day of summer unfolding. As the trees begin to evolve into their golden colors and the air is turning cooler, I am comforted by what I know. But my heart is also holding the memory of that mountain covered with snow and all the smaller mountains that ring the horizon of Seattle, hoping they continue to hold and inspire the adventure of this dear one of mine.

Scraps of Paper

We are here to abet creation and to witness to it, to notice each other's beautiful face and complex nature so that creation need not play to an empty house.   —Annie Dillard

I have a habit—some might call it a bad habit—of writing little cryptic notes to myself on small scraps of paper. Usually I put them in my pocket or slip them inside my date book or journal. I refer to them for ideas for writing, a sermon, or just because I found the words beautiful, important, inspiring. You get the idea. In most circumstances when I am finished using them in some way, I pitch them in the trash.

I was cleaning out some books of which I no longer have need, and this quote of Annie Dillard fell out of the book and onto the floor. Reaching down to pick it up, I read the words and a great smile spread across my face. This is a statement I have loved for a long time and I had forgotten it: "We are here to abet creation and to witness to it, to notice each other's beautiful face and complex nature so that creation need not play to an empty house." Let those words wash over you. Doesn't it give you a sense of purpose? Doesn't it fill you with some deep seeded joy? So, this is the answer to the question of why we are here!

I think I also love this phrase because it redeems the word "abet," meaning to support, encourage, approve, affirm. This is our work as humans: to encourage and support creation. This is our work: to approve the beauty of the faces of those we meet, to affirm the complex nature of the humans and non-humans in our lives. What if we gave ourselves this mission statement and set goals each day to accomplish the work of our lives? Can you imagine the change it might make in the world? It is a wonderful idea to imagine coming to fruition.

There are people I have met who seem to have known that this "abetting" stuff was their life's work. They are the ones who look you right in the eye as if you are the only person to whom they would want to talk in any particular moment. Their gaze causes you to stand taller, feel more confident, be more authentically yourself. These are the people who notice things—little things—that are good and comment on them. They are almost always the ones who send a little note out of the blue to tell you they enjoyed something you did, something you said.

Still other "abettors" I know are the ones who you will find standing quietly under a tree looking up into the branches, head tilted slightly to identify the song of a bird. They are the ones who can be seen showing a small child a tiny insect on the sidewalk, passing on the importance of the work of ants, spiders, even mosquitoes. They are the ones who can be seen gazing out toward a sunset with a far off look in their eyes as if trying to become a part of the mystery and beauty of that ending moment.

I want to become more of an "abettor," to follow the wisdom on this recovered scrap of paper. I want to do my work and do it well. I want to be the awe-struck audience member at this Universe play….. the one who doesn't rudely whisper to my neighbor, who doesn't rattle the candy wrapper making unneeded noise, who doesn't cough so incessantly that I distract those around me. I want to be present to the play, to offer fullness of my presence for all its worth, and when the time is perfect, applaud my appreciation.

Storm Home

Many years ago I remember sitting near the radio listening intently to "A Prairie Home Companion." Garrison Keillor's soft, soothing voice told of his childhood days in Lake Woebegon and his yearly assignment of a "storm home." The storm home was the place the children who lived in the country would go if the weather became too dangerous to go home. It was a beautiful story of the for which each of us longs, not only during storms but every day.

The light is on in the window in anticipation of our arrival. As the door is opened, we are welcomed in with joy. The fire is glowing warmly in the fireplace, delicious aromas float in the air . . . a promise of all our favorite comfort foods. After dinner, a bed stacked high with cozy warm blankets is waiting, and we are tucked in with love, a good story, and a prayer.

I think of this story when the snow is flying, the wind is blowing, and travel becomes more and more treacherous. Of course, Garrison's storm home is a fantasy created in his magnificent imagination. But it represents for each of us that iconic vision of home . . . that place where we will be safe, fed, warm, sheltered . . . but most of all welcomed unconditionally. It is an ideal for the majority of the world. We know that each day children are not welcomed into places of safety, adults are not well fed or held in loving care, and more people than we can imagine go to bed hungry and without anyone to tuck them in.

But that fact doesn't keep us from hoping, praying, longing for a storm home for all those people . . . and ourselves. Our collective prayers of compassion, followed by intentional action of some kind can and do make a difference, I believe—perhaps not in the larger system but in individual lives. Each time we make a donation, take food to the emergency food shelf, or volunteer at a shelter, we create a storm home for someone.

Most Christians have heard the story of the Prodigal Son in worship services. This story, I believe, holds so much of our faith story and our spiritual struggle. It holds the anticipation of personal freedom, a call to responsible living, our self-centeredness, our desire for adventure, the ability to get it right and at the same time oh-so-wrong. It tells of our selfishness and our creativity, our connection and desire to want to be "loved best." We could spend a whole year on this story and still be mining God's wisdom.

But above all, this story tells us that no matter what, no matter where, no matter how, no matter why, the Holy One is always present . . . with the light on, the meal prepared, arms outstretched, welcoming us with joy and unconditional love to our storm home.

Will you, God, really live with people on earth? Why, the heavens and their own heavens cannot contain you. How much less this house that I have built. . . . Listen to the cry and the prayer I make to you today, day and night let your eyes watch over this house, over this place of which you have said: My name shall be there.

—1 Kings 8:27-29

Psalm 95

Come, let us sing for joy to God;

> *let us shout aloud to the Rock of our salvation.*

Let us come before you with thanksgiving

> *and extol you with music and song.*

For you are the great God,

> *the great God above all gods.*

In your hand are the depths of the earth,

> *and the mountain peaks belong to you.*

The sea is yours, the Creator.

> *Holy hands formed the dry land.*

Squirrel Nests

When the trees are bare, stripped of their leaves by the winter wind, I become aware of the squirrel nests that dot the branches. All along our street the nests perch precariously high in the trees. The nests are not visible when the trees are full of leaves. But when the leaves are gone, there they are—resting between branches once full of green life, their cocoon of leaves and twigs and who know what else forming a home, a place to rest, give birth, and grow.

I can't imagine what a squirrel thinks, but from a human perspective it seems to me that building a nest closer to the center of the tree makes more sense. It would be much safer. I find myself thinking: Why does the nest need to be so high, out on such a thin limb? And yet, I know I have certainly built many "homes" in some very difficult and dangerous places. As humans we often choose to rest and grow in places where there is great opportunity and yet great peril. It is the choice of adventurers and seekers to go to the edge, to seek the opportunity to grow in a variety of new ways. Perhaps it is the practice of going back and forth to their nests that allows squirrels to run across the telephone lines with the skill of an acrobat, never falling, always making a straight shot from point A to point B. An admirable ability for both human and squirrel!

Where we build our nests can help us grow or challenge us to new feats of adventure. Where we build our nests can instill courage and daring or invite us to leap with faith. I once had a card hanging on my office door that read "Leap . . . and the net will appear." That must be the mantra of squirrels and all those who build their nests on limbs that seem fragile to the casual observer.

Where are you building your nest these days? Is your life calling you to build higher, go out on a limb so to speak, take the contents of your nest to the edge? Or are you carrying the materials you need, comfortably perhaps, to a safer place to hunker down against the winter wind near the sturdy trunk of the tree and be present in a quieter more contemplative way? The good news is that life calls for both.

There Are Days

There are days that are more vibrant than others. They are filled with moments that make you want to shout your praise for simply being alive. Colors are brighter, smells sweeter, the eyes of a friend shine out at you from a face you love but have taken for granted. The arms of a partner are warmer, gentler than you can remember, and you want to spend the day resting in their embrace. There are days like this.

Many times these days are brought on by a wonderful miraculous experience—like the birth of a new baby or the news that something you've worked on for so long has come to fruition. But more often these days are brought on because you feel you've brushed close to having the gifts of this life snatched away from you. You pass by the scene of an accident where there are clearly grave injuries. Or you yourself stop or swerve just in time to miss being part of a similar scene. Test results that come back clear, and phone messages signal the joyous voice of a family member or friend over this good news. There are days like this.

We spend the majority of our time treading the waters of our lives. It is a fact and one that, in some ways, makes the world go round. We find ourselves in the rhythm of routines that can dull our senses and our hearts to the sheer joy of walking this glorious earth. We go to meetings, do the laundry, eat a meal without paying attention to the food or our companions. And then something happens, and our awareness changes. Our senses become heightened, and our eyes see the world as if for the first time. There are days like this.

Perhaps it is the nature of being human, of trying to make sense of who we are, that allows us to become aware of these luminous experiences when we recognize the gift of this life, this living. Do other animals feel the exhilaration of having outrun the hand of death in the form of the speeding car? Do they then enjoy their running or flying or swimming more for at least the next few days? I don't know.

Wherever you are, whatever you are doing, today might be a day to really look around you and see the gifts of your life. Today might be the day to smile broader, to kiss longer, to order dessert, to give a gift anonymously. Today might be a day to fall in love with your life . . . without benefit of any dramatic event . . . but simply because you can.

Walking on Water

The people realized that God was at work among them in what Je-
sus had just done. They said, "This is the Prophet for sure, God's
Prophet right here in Galilee!" Jesus saw that in their enthusiasm,
they were about to grab him and make him king, so he slipped off
and went back up the mountain to be by himself. In the evening
the disciples went down to the seas, got in the boat, and headed
back across the water to Capernaum. It had grown quite dark
and Jesus had not yet returned. A huge wind blew up, churning
the sea. They were maybe three or four miles out when they saw
Jesus walking on the sea, quite near the boat. They were scared
senseless, but he reassured them, "It's me, it's all right. Don't be
afraid." So they took him on board. In no time they reached land
on the exact spot they were headed to.

—John 6:14-21, *The Message*

The sunset over the lake was breathtaking. I stood with my companions looking out the large windows that face the water as the sky
turned from blue to lavender, then pink to orange and yellow, painting
a palette worthy of any Impressionist artist. How does it happen? Why
does it happen?

I don't know the answer to those questions, but I know what the
result is: awe, wonder, a sense of being present for something so much
bigger than myself that I must stop and take note of it, perhaps breathing out a prayer of gratitude.

On the frozen lake, the ice houses dot the landscape with color . . .
reds, blues, yellows . . . tiny structures floating on water. Sitting beside the houses, trucks, cars, and four-wheelers are ready for a quick
or leisurely get-away, an exit most likely driven by the windchill that
sweeps across the lake. It is a truly Minnesota scene. There are few
other places on the planet where people don't blink at such a sight.
Houses, cars, lives being lived out . . . held up by water.

The ancients believed that evil lurked below the surface of water,
things unseen over which humans have no power. So the stories of Jesus walking on water showed his power to overcome the fears that can
grip us. As he walked toward the disciples they knew that he indeed
was the prophet they had longed for, the one who could over turn the
tables of injustice, the one who could release them from their fear of
the most unseen thing of all . . . death. He walked with confidence on
the surface of what had the potential to swallow them up.

On the frozen Minnesota lake, suspended between the awe and majesty of the Creator's artistic hand, people sit now. They may not be having any particularly transcendent moment or thinking thoughts about overcoming evil, but I bet they are sure having fun. And God is at work in that, too.

Psalm 104

Praise God, O my soul.

    O my God, you are very great;

    you are clothed with splendor and majesty.

You are wrapped in light as with a garment;

    and you stretch out the heavens like a tent

and lay the beams of the upper chambers

    on their waters.

You make the clouds a chariot

    and ride on the wings of the wind.

You make the winds messengers;

    flames of fire are your servants.

You set the earth on its foundations;

    it can never be moved.

You covered it with the deep as with a garment;

    the waters stood above the mountains.

Blaze Orange

I headed out for a long walk through the winter woods. The paths are groomed and easy to follow as they wind through the now bare birch trees. The towering evergreens provide the only color against the deep blue of sky. As I laced up my boots and put on my heavy coat, I also followed the directions taped to the door: "Remember to wear your orange vest when leaving!" I reached for the blaze orange which would make me visible to any hunters who may still be out. Though the hunting season is over, so I was told, there are still some who might be about. Putting aside any fashion sense, I zipped up this big, florescent vest and began my silent pilgrimage.

The path led me past fallen trees that had been arranged to make the path more visible. I thought of how lovely it would be with more snow to offer the contrast to the pines and birch. As I walked I was aware of how conspicuous I felt. It was like I was shouting, "Look at me! Look at me!" It had not been my intention when I planned this woodland walk. I had wanted, instead, to become a part of the woods, to become a part of the fabric of the forest. But my vest made me "other." There was no mistaking that an alien was present in the natural landscape. While I was safe, I also felt sad to not have blended into and become part of the beauty of the woods, of the earth.

Walking out of the woods, I made my way to the open field where people had built a rock and prairie grass labyrinth for walking prayer. An ornamental archway marks the opening of the labyrinth. Attached to the archway hangs a small brass pine cone bell. I gently rang it to signal my entrance. I began my slow, meditative walk offering prayers for family, friends, the work my colleagues and I were doing here at the retreat center. I reached the center of the labyrinth and the small pile of stones where people had left smaller stones, an angel was imprinted on a coin with John 3:16 printed on it—visible talismans of their own prayers. Nestled within the larger stones were pieces of paper. I resisted the impulse to pull them out and read them, believing they were meant for the Holy and not for me. As I stood at the center of this ancient path, my eyes fell on the brightness of my vest. At first I wanted to laugh . . . walking the labyrinth in blaze orange! It seemed so silly.

And yet what my heart wanted was for my prayers, for my walk, for my living, to be noticed by the One who holds me gently in this life's path. And in that spirit, blaze orange seemed the perfect attire.

O God, you have searched me and known me. You know when I sit down and when I rise up; you discern my thoughts from far away. You search out my path and my lying down, and are acquainted with all my ways. Even before a word is on my tongue, you know it completely. You hem me in, behind and before, and lay your hand upon me.

—Psalm 139

Tikkun alam

In the Jewish mystic tradition of Kabbalah, the creation story begins with God's creating the world by filling a container that will hold the universe. God continues to fill and doesn't stop pouring until the container itself explodes and the universe—and God—gets broken into tiny pieces flying all over the place. In this tradition, it is the work of humanity to take the shattered pieces and *tikkun alam*, "repair the world," remembering that God is also contained in the broken pieces.

I have always loved this creation story. It speaks of a God who got carried away with creation and the Holy that lives in even the tiniest of its pieces. It is probably why I have always loved certain kinds of art . . . mosaics, collage, weaving . . . anything that takes smaller pieces and brings them together to make something bigger, more whole, more beautiful.

One such artist was Lillian Colton, a favorite of those who spend time at the Minnesota State Fair. Lillian's art could be found in the horticulture building. The medium of her art: seeds. Ninety-five when she died, Lillian spent years taking the tiniest of seeds and creating portraits of famous people using only natural elements. It was a yearly tradition for our family to try to guess who Lillian would immortalize in seed for this year's fair. Lillian, who was often present at the fair near her artwork, sometimes talked with viewers, other times worked diligently on yet another project.

I don't know anything about Lillian's motivation for her work. Growing up on a farm, it might have just been a natural thing to do. But I know for me, the beauty of it was somehow connected to *tikkun alam*, the work of taking the small, individual shards of seed and bringing them together to create a fuller, more complete picture. These seeds—which contain the ability to grow and even bring life—are in truth filled with the goodness of God.

How might we go about the work of "repairing the world" if we remembered that indeed the Holy resides in each and every seed, atom, cell, plant, creature, human, relationship? How might we go about taking the smallest step in repairing the world if we remembered that in that action we also come to know God more wholly and fully as well?

Today, I give thanks for Lillian's long, full life . . . and for her yearly reminder of how the tiniest of elements of God's creation can come together to make the fullest of pictures. May I, may each of us, have the courage to help *tikkun alam*, in our own unique ways.

Shells

The sea does not reward those who are too anxious, too greedy, or too impatient. One should lie empty, open, choiceless as a beach— waiting for a gift from the sea.

—Anne Morrow Lindbergh, *Gift from the Sea*

At each beach, I started out telling myself that I would only pick up the very unusual one. But before I knew it there I was, pockets full, hands full, no more room . . . until the next walk. On this outing the only thing missing was the occasional addition of the shell that one of my sons knew I couldn't live without. Off on their own adventures now, I missed their contributions to my obsession.

I have spent the last several days on beaches. Some were filled with retired folks walking leisurely with seemingly not a care in the world. On others college students played volleyball and Frisbee, full of the exuberance of spring break in a warm climate. Peppered among these people were families with young children building sand castles and trying to outrun the waves as they rolled onto shore. And there were plenty of us who fell in between all these descriptions.

The common bond of all these people? Shells. All along the beaches people of varying ages and stages of life periodically bent over and retrieved from the sand a treasure . . . a sea shell. What is the amazing appeal of these fragile things? Is it the tiny, unique, and intricate beauty of each one? Is it that they were once home to something living? Is it that they somehow connect us with the sea, that place from which humans emerged to walk the earth? I have gathered shells from beaches that washed up from both the Atlantic and Pacific Oceans. I have also carried in my sandy pockets shells from lakes, both great and small. These gifts of the water are formed into little altars both inside and outside our home. No matter one's view of the genesis of creation, all humans came into the world through the water that held us . . . our mother's womb. Our first home was water, and the majority of our body is made up of water. So it only seems right that we should walk the sand and recover these little containers of life that were once held in the vastness of water.

At baptism we often use shells to remind us of the vast bodies of water that nurture us, nourish us, connect us, cleanse us, give us life. This earth on which we travel is mostly water, a shell of sorts on which we ride, tucked into its curves and crannies. We listen for the *whoosh* of its water within our ears, within our heart. We grow and outgrow, abandon our shell homes, and take on new ones. Yet this earth home remains constant, true. Perhaps that is what draws us to these jewels we find when the tides deliver them at our feet. Bending down, we reach out and pick up and we remember. Young ones new to this earth tuck an oyster shell in a pocket and remember. Those full of the promise of what is yet to be press a scallop shell into the hand of another young one and remember. Reaching down and saving a conch shell from being drawn back into the tide, those who have walked the beach many years remember.

And so it goes . . . on and on and on.

Sightseeing

You're not going to see people like this again for a long time, he
said & I said I always saw people like this & he looked at me for a
moment & said, You're not from around here, are you?
—Brian Andreas, *Traveling Light*

Back on Minnesota soil, surrounded by the blinding light of sun
on snow, I have found myself daydreaming about last week's trip to
the beach. I have been caught staring longingly off into the distance,
remembering the green grass, brilliant colors of flowers, warm temperatures, sumptuous food I didn't cook and the slow pace that usually
overtakes a person when they have the sound of surf as their background music.

I have also been thinking about the interesting people we met and
those we only observed. One young woman in particular keeps coming to mind. Thursday afternoon we walked the sand on Hilton Head
Island. People were running, riding bikes, flying kites, reading, and
just sitting—soaking up the sun. I was walking with my head turned
toward the water. That's when I saw the first fin move above the
waves. Soon there was another and another, and then people stopped
to watch. Dolphins!

As we stood there staring, my eyes were diverted by a young
woman in a bathing suit and tank shirt, camera in hand. She was
walking in a way that was so determined I had to stop looking at the
dolphins and watch her. Her long, lithe strides took her right into the
icy, cold water, her arms now lifted high above her head to keep the
camera dry. She was so focused, so intent on getting as close as hu-
manly possible, I began to feel this affinity with her desire. Inside my
head I was cheering her on. "Go, go, swim as near as you can. . . . swim
with the dolphins!"

The beautiful mammals moved down the beach, following the
wind and waves. Someone called out to her, "Look, there they are!"
She was now an extension of all who watched. But she was the brave
one, moving through the waves, the water nearly up to her neck. She
was close to them now, but they of course kept moving while she was
constantly pushed back by the power of the waves, held nearly in place
by the power of the undertow.

Back on the land, a woman dressed in warmer clothes called her
name. *Her mother?* Finally, she began to move back toward shore.
Did she get the picture she wanted? Did she get close enough? I don't

know. Somehow as I left that scene I was certain of one thing. I am sure that was not the first time the one who called her name had seen the determined, confident walk that led her into the sea. A smile began to form on my face . . . and I stood a little taller. In this young woman I sensed all the times I had boldly stepped into deep waters to reach for what seemed most important and yet fleeting. Her determination echoed within me as I harnessed once again a power I had perhaps forgotten: the focused power to reach for what may never come again and to seize the moment that is before me.

> *I hope it will be said we taught them to stand tall & proud, even in the face of history & the future was made new & whole for us all, one child at a time.* —Brian Andreas

Standing Watch

For several days, I have been standing watch. Standing watch over the cherry bush given by a circle of friends as a memorial gift at the time of my father's death. Since we planted it the summer after his passing, it has always bloomed on a day near the anniversary of his death, April 23. But not this year. This year there were no visible buds on the bush. The cold and gray of a lingering winter held it back from its delicate, perfect pink flowers. And so I have been watching and waiting.

When April 23 rolled around and I could see that there would be no flowers for this anniversary, I was at first a little angry. Then I felt sadness and disappointment. It had meant something special to have those flowers bloom as homage to my dad who was a great lover of cherry pie. But as the time wore on I began to see this delay for what it really was . . . a reminder that things don't always happen when they are "supposed" to. Some plants (like some people) take longer to grow and flourish than others; some seasons last longer than we'd like, while others move on far too quickly.

I thought of the many times I have willed a project or situation to move forward, to progress, to "do something!" only to be made to practice patience and the humbling act of tongue-biting. If every parent or teacher could have a nickel for every child they have wanted to suc-ceed more quickly, mature faster, only to learn—or re-learn—that all children do best when growing and moving at their own pace . . . why think of the fortunes we'd amass!

Yesterday afternoon when I came home in the rain, I looked out the window to see that some buds had reached a fullness. With today's sunshine, I am happy to say the bush has finally begun to flower. It has taken nearly three weeks longer than other years, but over the next few days everyone who passes by our house will have the blessing of the sight of this sweet, little bush.

The cherry bush is blooming in its own sweet time, following the wisdom and rhythm of sun, rain, and temperature. To have brought forth those lovely blossoms earlier would have meant a certain wilting death. Unlike its human guard, the plant knew exactly what to do and the right time to do it. How much I have learned from this precious plant!

Over the next few days I will continue to stand watch, realizing that *now* is the appropriate time to do what humans were meant to do

. . . be awestruck with the beauty and wonder of it all and give thanks. The cherry bush will do its job, and I will do mine, and all will be right with the world.

> *Silently a flower blooms, in silence it falls away; yet here now, at this moment, at this place, the world of the flower, the whole of the world is blooming. This is the talk of the flower, the truth of the blossom; the glory of eternal life is fully shining here.*
>
> —Zenkei Shibayama

Matthew 6:26

Look at the birds of the air; they neither sow nor reap nor gather into barns, and yet your heavenly Creator feeds them. Are you not of more value than they?

Rutabaga

I am about to do a new thing; now it springs forth, do you not perceive it?
— Isaiah 43:19

It started with a recipe for a hearty root vegetable soup. Sometime in January I had found the perfect soup for a winter day, so I went to the grocery store and purchased all the ingredients. I came home and put everything away, and one thing led to another and I never got around to making the soup. The sweet potatoes were used as a quick dinner one evening. The acorn squash was baked with butter and orange juice. The carrots were eaten as a snack. The onions found their way into a salad or as topping for a sandwich.

But the rutabaga languished under the kitchen sink in the dark. Several days ago I came downstairs to see it sitting on the kitchen table. It had been found by my husband as he rooted (sorry about that) around under the sink for something. The rutabaga, perhaps one of the least lovely vegetables, had sprouted beautiful, frilly deep green leaves. While resting in the dark, this peasant vegetable had become a lovely sight. Right now it is sitting in our kitchen window continuing to amaze us with its foliage.

When I think of rutabagas I often think of the memoirs I have read about World War II. It seems this vegetable often made the base of many soups that kept prisoners alive. The vegetable, for me, holds a certain sadness and stark quality for that very reason. And yet, here it is right now, bringing such pleasure.

So many times in our lives we are confronted with people or situations that seem to be without beauty like the lowly rutabaga, without much hope for being more than a knobby, hopeless eyesore. I am sure that as most of us pass by the person standing at the street corner, sign in hand, asking for help, we do not see the fullness of cauliflower or the delicacy of a vine-ripened tomato. Yet, I believe that within each person, within each difficult situation, there is the potential to bring forth new life, something unseen and yet to be realized. In other words, to see as God sees. Isn't that the core message of the resurrection story?

In those days which hold the joy of Easter, we are called to look for signs that, indeed, Life exists at the center of all. And so we can walk, if we choose, through the world with eyes wide open, watching for the presence of the Sacred in our midst . . . even, perhaps especially, in the lowly rutabaga. And doesn't that deserve an "Alleluia!"?

Lily of the Valley

I have found a friend in Jesus, he's everything to me,
He's the fairest of ten thousand to my soul.
He's the Lily of the Valley, he's the bright and Morning Star,
He's the fairest of ten thousand to my soul.

I could only remember a snippet of this old hymn so I had to go searching for it today. I remember singing it as a child, mostly at hymn sing gatherings on hot, humid, summer Sunday nights. The ceiling fans of St. Paul's United Methodist Church turned lazily in the summer heat, and we all fanned ourselves as we sang. We could work up quite a sweat singing those old hymns!

I'm not sure I understood the reference to Jesus as "lily of the valley" at the time, but the song had a great tune and I liked singing it. I later learned that a legend says that, while standing at the cross, Mary, Jesus' mother, wept. As she did her tears fell, and lilies of the valley sprang from the ground. That story must have been an inspiration for the hymn writer. All I knew was I liked thinking of Jesus as this sweet, fragrant flower. After all, wasn't lily of the valley May's flower, my birthday flower?

Those dainty, bell-like flowers, surrounded by such out of proportion leaves, show themselves in spring. Our side yard, which is shaded by large evergreens, produces more and more of them each year. A walk in our yard yields their very particular scent, simple and pure, a sure sign that summer is just around the corner.

The white flowers don't last long; their season is short. If you get distracted or are busy doing other May things, of which there are many, you can miss them all together. Perhaps their sweetness is intensified by their short life, their simplicity, their lack of showiness. After all, they are a hardy flower with deep roots that form extensive colonies by spreading underground. They like to reach out and grow in places that other flowers don't, can't, won't. They fight their way into the world through cold and ice, reaching toward the sun. They could go unnoticed if a person's eyes were looking the other way, if their heart was not open to them.

Jesus . . . Lily of the Valley . . . it has taken some years, but maybe I get it now.

R U My Mother?

I have several friends who are doulas, those who are trained to be companions at pregnancy and birth. I am amazed by their work and by their stories of being witnesses to the birth of another new one who will walk this earth. It is work that, I imagine, takes patience, wisdom, deep relationship, trust, and a large dose of hope. I send blessings and prayers for all those engaged in this holy companioning.

Our family has been, in a sense, acting as doulas over the last several weeks as we have kept watch over a nest built in the tree that is adjacent to an upstairs window. When we noticed it, we saw only the fat mother robin now sitting there. When the robin flew away from the nest, I climbed into the attic to peer down to see if there were indeed any eggs nestled within. There, fragile and brilliant blue, lay one single egg. Within moments the mother was back and settled in. Over the days that followed, we observed the father bringing food to the nest and heard raucous sounds as a crow was chased away until finally my climb once more into the attic produced a glimpse of a pitiful, ugly, little squirming mass.

Winds were strong over the next days, and yet the mother sat tight on her offspring, shielding it from cold and the chance of being blown to its death. It was at that moment that I remembered a book our boys had loved as children. It was titled *Are You My Mother?* It told the story of a baby bird who had fallen out of the nest and went searching for its mother. The bird would approach other living things, a dog and an owl, asking "Are you my mother?" Throughout the story, of course, there were near misses with danger until finally the baby bird came to a steel crane and asked, "Are you my mother?" The large machine gave no answer but slowly lifted the baby bird back into the nest where it was reunited with the mother who had been searching for it.

The reality of course is that there was really nothing our family did to help this little bird born in our tree to enter the world. The ways of creation have provided for that. But we felt somehow connected to these harbingers of spring, these feathered ones we look for so ardently in April and May. We kept watch and became witness to the fragility of their lives. I would love to think that, had the winds blown the baby from its nest, we could have been like the crane and returned it safely to the presence of its mother.

But there was no need. This morning I saw the robin, now looking more adolescent than infant, scraggly feathers poking out from its growing body. The mother was not home, and the bird was walking with a feigned confidence around the edge of the nest. It was waiting to fly.

As a mother, I know that look. It is one that fills our hearts with fear and pride and resignation. It is a reminder that the real job of parenting is to give our children roots. . . and wings. Blessed be the handiwork. Blessed be. Blessed be.

Earth Home

Seek the beginnings, learn from whence you came, and know the various earth of which you are made.
—Edwin Muir, Scottish poet, from "The Journey"

Is there a place you long for, a literal place where you seem more at home than any other? Have you ever arrived in a new town or a place in the country and had that feeling of having come "home"? Is there a lake or a mountain that floats into your consciousness during the day, at the oddest of times, and brings you deep connection and deep peace?

There is an older movie, *A Trip to Bountiful*, in which a woman longs so deeply for her childhood farm that rests near the town of Bountiful; she makes a pilgrimage there. She takes off, without the knowledge of her doting children, and makes her way back to Bountiful and the land that had been permanently imprinted in her memory, in her body, in her cells. She moves about the house and the land with a deep reverence, touching with gratitude all that is around her. In her waning years, she knew she must make a reconnection with the ground where she was shaped, the ground that held her life.

If we allow ourselves, we can become aware of those places that call to us . . . those that connect in deeper ways than others . . . to the very heart of our being. Sometimes these places are literally the home where we were born, our birthplace, and sometimes they are the land of our ancestors. If we have the privilege to travel, we can often see how our ancestors that came to this country settled in areas that looked a great deal like those they left behind. The first time I traveled to Wales I was struck with how much the countryside in southern Ohio, my birthplace, looked like the Welsh hills. When I traveled to Norway, I was aware of the similarities between northern Minnesota and the lush, yet rugged land of that Scandinavian country.

Where is your Bountiful? Where is the place that calls to your heart over and over? Where is your true earth home? Perhaps these places call to us in the way they do because we most fully experience the Holy there. Perhaps these places are our memory of Eden . . . that place where we knew the true blessings of our home with God.

May this day bring you the experience of your true earth home . . . if not literally . . . then in rich memory.

Yet still from Eden springs the root, as clean as on the starting day.
—Edwin Muir

Lots of Lettuce

This is why we do it all again every year. It's the visible daily growth, the marvelous and unaccountable accumulation of biomass that makes for the hallelujah of a July garden.
—Barbara Kingsolver in *Animal, Vegetable, Miracle: A Year of Food Life*

We purchased a share in a community sustainable agriculture farm. Through a friend who knows the farmers, we plopped down some cash—"seed money," excuse the pun—to be part of group of people who receive fresh, organic vegetables on a weekly basis. Every Thursday evening we drive into a parking lot, pull up to a little, blue station wagon that is loaded with coolers. Out of the back of the car a friendly face calls out our name, and we step forward to receive a bag of surprises. I have often wondered what passersby think as they see us. What are those people doing? Is it legal?

Farming is tricky business. You plant and so many variables play into what you harvest . . . sun, rain, heat, wind, storms, drought. It is a wonderful metaphor for so much of life. Since late May we have received mostly bags of leafy vegetables . . . spinach, dill and other herbs, lamb's ear, clover, greens, and lots and lots of lettuce. While we tend to eat lots of salads, it is almost impossible to get through all the lettuce in one week—and then, alas, more lettuce! The bounty can be staggering.

Last night, however, as I held my hand out with humility, I noticed the weight of the bag . . . heavy. Green leafiness protruded from the bag, but there had to be something else with all that weight. I could hardly wait to get home to see what was inside. As I unloaded the bag onto the kitchen table, pushing aside still more lettuce, I found a gleaming white onion, a clump of brilliant red onions, bright red beets still fresh with earth, tiny perfect cherry tomatoes, and fragrant basil. The heaviest vegetables had, of course, fallen to the bottom of the bag . . . zucchini . . . both yellow and green. Knowing the prolific nature of this versatile squash, my mind projected ahead to what the next weeks will bring.

This collaboration with the farmers and others is about so much more than receiving the vegetables each week. It is about knowing the people who grow the food we put on the table and being thankful for their work. It is about knowing that the lettuce I love did not take thousands of gallons of fossil fuel to get to our table. It is about the conversation and camaraderie that happens in the parking lot. And it is about the surprise, about receiving the offering of what the earth, through the labor and love of those who planted and harvested, had to offer this week, in this season.

And so as the month continues to unfold, I know there will be more and more zucchini, and we will be challenged and blessed with finding new and different ways to prepare it. Barring a drastic shift in the weather, the bounty will continue to grow, because that is the nature of summer in Minnesota. We will continue to drive into the parking lot and be handed our bag of nutritious surprises. And then it will begin to trickle off once again just as it began, and it will be time to put on warmer clothes, prepare our houses for winter, and close our doors to the bounty we have known.

The good news is that behind those closed doors, people will be poring over seed catalogues, planning for next summer, next July . . . and more lettuce.

Solved?

The news reports carried headlines declaring "Northern Lights Mysteries Revealed." This week NASA "released findings that indicate magnetic explosions about one-third of the way to the moon cause the northern lights, or aurora borealis, to burst into spectacular shapes and colors, and dance across the sky." The scientists have their reasons for trying to solve the mystery of this amazing night show. One reason is the hope of developing ways of knowing how geomagnetic storms disrupt the satellites in orbit that no doubt power many of the things upon which we now rely. I am . . . in my very, very, non-scientific mind . . . thinking this means things like cell phones, digital television, and GPS systems.

Truth be told, I have been just fine not having any clue how it all happens. How the sky can fill with green and red and purple shoots of light that undulate and move with the grace of Fred Astaire across the sky, accompanied by that faint piercing hum of an other worldly music—I have been satisfied with the miracle of it all. Truth be told, I might be more likely to sing along with songwriter Iris Dement: "*Everybody's wonderin' what and where they all came from. Everybody's worryin' 'bout where they're gonna go when the whole thing's done. But no one knows for certain and so it's all the same to me. I think I'll just let the mystery be.*"

I still remember the first time I ever saw the Northern Lights. It was a late summer evening on what is known as the "upper field" at Koinonia retreat center, just west of Annandale, Minnesota. Walking up the hill, I noticed the humming first, a high, faint pitch that permeated the air. I have to admit I found it a bit unnerving. What could possibly be making such a sound? When I came to the top of the hill and onto the flat surface of the parking lot, people were already standing there, looking toward the horizon and the ballet of color that was moving with wild abandon across the sky. No one spoke. How could we? We were held in the smallness of what it means to be humans witnessing something bordering on the miraculous. Since that time I have seen the aurora borealis only twice more. I pray my life has a few more opportunities left in it.

Scientists have their reasons for solving mysteries, and we have all reaped the rewards of their research. I am thankful for their gifts, their education, and their curiosity. But as for me, I am content with the wonder and awe of the Mystery.

Water Like Glass

I sat on large boulders on the beach at Grand Marais having my morning coffee. If one is an early riser as I am, you learn how to make an escape wherever you are staying without waking your fellow travelers. Tiptoeing out the door after silently making the coffee, I would make my way down the hill toward Lake Superior. I would sit and simply stare at the contemplative yet breathtaking scene before me . . . colorful fishing boats out on the glassy water, gulls flying in lace-like patterns in the air, no doubt hoping for an easy breakfast. Besides the fishermen, only a few other people were awake, walking dogs that had been held captive by the night. One or two dogless people . . . also early risen escapees . . . ran or walked along the shore. The only sound that graced the morning was the faint hum of the boat motors and the incessant call of the gulls.

At one point my eyes moved from the shining surface of the water to meet the gaze of a woman walking leisurely by: "It is so calming, isn't it? So calming. . . ." In monosyllables, I agreed. Nothing more was necessary. We both returned our vision to the mirror of water that reflected the sky and the dome of blue it created. So calming. . . .

What is it about water that attracts us? Is it the deep realization that we once swam in the womb waters of our mothers? Or, like the sea creatures from which we evolved, do we somehow know that we all once swam in the womb of God? And the calmness that can come over us, does it stem from the wisdom that water is at the center of all the deepest myths that live in our memory . . . all the many creation stories from which the Holy One stills the chaotic, frightful waters and brings forth abundant life?

I don't know the answer to these very big questions. All I know is that when I sit, when I allow myself to meditate upon the ebb and flow of the waters of lake or ocean, river or stream, something causes my heart to slow to a regular, healthy rhythm, and the pressure of the blood coursing through my veins becomes even. "It's so calming, isn't it?" Yes, yes it is. So calming.

Fog

*Neither the pillar of cloud by day nor the pillar of fire by night left
its place in front of the people.* —Exodus 13:22

I woke early. Looking out the window of a friend's home just a few
feet from the shore of Lake Superior, I saw the fog that was enveloping
everything as far as the eye could see. I was drawn to it.

Getting up and making the coffee which would warm my hands
as I cradled it in the cool morning air, I headed just a few blocks away
toward the beach. The gulls circled someplace overhead though I knew
them only by the sound of their voices. Nearly everything was invisible in the density of the grounded clouds. Now sensing only its deep
presence I stood looking out toward what, the night before, had been
only clear, dark blue waters. I stood shrouded in the fog looking out
toward the horizon, the shifting stones of the beach crunching under
my feet. I realized I was holding my breath as I waited for some sound,
something to become visible to me, some affirmation that I was not
alone.

As the sun began to lighten the morning sky, the fog gave way,
and the outline of a yellow sailboat caught my eye. Out in the distance
the sound of a ship's signal awakened my senses further. I had no
idea how near or how distant the path it was traveling on the big lake,
Gitchi Gumee. Someplace out there on the deck of a ship headed to who
knows where, someone may have been looking back toward me as
I looked longingly for their outline against the ever brightening sky.
Enveloped in the stillness, unable to recognize anything that would
give me anchor, I could have felt frightened. And yet, instead, what I
heard was the still small voice within. Though my eyes could not make
out another single, living soul, I knew I was held safe. I was receiving
the message I had so many times before: "Do not be afraid. You are not
alone."

The thought crossed my mind: This is often how it feels in my
experience of the Holy One. I stand in a fog, straining with the eyes
behind my eyes to see the outline of the One who is as near as the
breath I am holding. Out in the distance that Presence, made visible in
my gently rising chest, signals to me: "Here I am, here I am." I exhale. I
inhale. Knowing, deeply knowing.

Harvesting Wind

Driving down Interstate 35 through Iowa, looking out into the corn and soybean fields, I cannot help but be impressed by the wind turbines standing straight and tall on the horizon. There is a majestic nature to their very presence, the blades turning slowly, making the watcher aware of the invisible . . . wind. I cannot even fathom how they really work. They are pure mystery to me and, it seems, pure economic and ecological genius to those who own the land on which they stand. The whole idea of "harvesting wind" to create energy, electricity, is a powerful concept, an even more powerful metaphor.

In the Pentecost story told in Acts, the Holy Spirit is described as a rushing wind. That wind blows through the people, and their lives are forever changed, their community is infused with energy . . . electricity . . . and their faith becomes a source that draws people to them and fuels their lives. They move from being a group of ordinary people to an extraordinary community. In a sense, they also were "harvesting wind."

Do you remember those little pinwheels you had as a child? It was a straw or stick with a colorful paper or plastic wheel which you'd blow on or hold into the wind, watching the air catch the colors and turn them into a spinning, whirling, rainbow blur. It was such a simple toy . . . but what fun! The invisible source . . . sometimes caused by your own hot air . . . caused this static thing to become beautiful movement.

Perhaps that is what the Spirit longs to be for us . . . that invisible Source that causes the static places in our lives, in our communities, in our world to become beautiful movement. Like the wind turbines hovering on the edges of the freeway or the pinwheel in our hands, the Spirit continues to offer a creative, creating energy for our lives. Infused with that Spirit, we become agents of change, co-creators with the Holy. As we harvest the wind of the Spirit, our lives can be transformed in ways that have the power to heal the world. All we need do is remember to connect to that Source.

The wind blows wherever it pleases. You hear its sound, but you cannot tell where it comes from or where it is going. So it is with everyone born of the Spirit.
—John 3

Letting Go

When I let go of what I am, I become what I might be. —Lao Tzu

A friend told me that, as she spent time having her morning coffee, she had watched the leaves fall from the tree near her deck. She remarked, "As I watched them let go, I wondered what I needed to let go of. What am I holding on to that needs to be released?" It is a great metaphor, a great question. And I love the idea that it was the wisdom of that tree that birthed the big question in her mind.

Of course in telling me her story, the question got passed on as these things often do and so now I, too, have been asking myself this question. "What do I need to let go of?" Outside my office window the enormous oak tree is in a curious state: some leaves very brown, others yellowing, still others are as green as July. Obviously this tree represents varied states of letting go. It echoes the state of being human—a perpetual balance of holding on and letting go. We do this daily, weekly, yearly, on and on. There are parts of our lives that will be going along just fine, and we have no need to release a thing. But other parts are yellowing and need to continue to turn brown . . . and finally let go.

Letting go is a scary thing. As I watched a leaf fall slowly to the ground, I wondered about its fall. Will the landing be soft, gentle? Will it collide with the gravel and get scratched up? Will it fall into the cold water that still stands from an earlier rain? Will it land on the playground equipment and get carried away on the shoe of a child playing beneath the giant tree? Letting go . . . a scary but necessary thing for growth. I know this lesson from watching this same tree for many years.

And so I ask myself again . . . and I ask you . . . what things must be "let go" to make room for the growth that is to come? How might each of us learn from the wisdom of the trees that each year release the life that has been in order to embrace what is yet to be?

These are big questions for our very big lives.

First

First you need only look:
Notice and honor the radiance of
Everything about you. . . .
Play in this universe. Tend
All these shining things around you:
The smallest plant, the creatures and
Objects in your care.
Be gentle and nurture. Listen. . . .
As we experience and accept
All that we really are. . . .
We grow in care.   —Anne Hillman

I write this from a favorite coffee shop that overlooks the backwaters of the Mississippi River. I come here when I need to sit on "my perch" as I refer to it . . . a tall chair at the back window. Outside the window the shop owner has placed several bird feeders. If I sit still enough and am not dressed in clothing that is too bright, I can remain observant less than a foot away from the birds as they feed their tiny bodies. Already this morning the chickadees and gold finches have been busily having breakfast as I have been having mine. Over the span of time I have come to this chair I have seen countless birds, observed them in the trees below and at very close proximity. It is a form of meditation for me, hugging a warm cup of coffee with my hands, sitting as still as I possibly can, and looking eye to eye (that's how it seems) with these beautiful, fragile, vulnerable creatures.

Sitting this close, I can observe the ones who've "done battle" in some way . . . their feathers are missing in places. I think of those people I know who have a similar look. Life has not treated them kindly. (*A nut hatch has just arrived.*) I can also see closely those who are the "thrivers" . . . those who manage to escape any of life's hard knocks with the fullness of their feathers intact. I think also of those humans I know who seem to live a charmed life—no ruffled feathers for them. This morning I send my blessing to all of these.

Recently I sat with a group of friends viewing a DVD by the cosmologist Brian Swimme. Its title was *The Power of the Universe*. It was a fascinating lecture about the interconnectedness of the universe, our place as humans in it, and the message of what it means to live at this time in the history of our planet. It was dense material, but I walked away from it all with a sense of hope, a sense of potential, a sense that, indeed, we are living at a unique and important time.(*Crows are keeping watch from the tree tops.*) We are being called to be caregivers of this amazing home in very significant ways that will have an impact on the future, not only for our children and grandchildren, but also for all the species, both plant and animal, that share in our living.

Somehow watching these tiny winged ones confirms this. . . . We are inextricably connected with one another in this sacred web. (*A flock of geese just made their way down river.*) So today I will take a step in what I hope is the right direction. I take this moment to honor the radiance out this window . . . the birds, the river, the tree . . . and the humans who share this comfy coffeehouse. And so *first,* may my steps . . . may yours . . . be gentle and nurturing, and may we grow in care, honoring the creation and the Creator by our living.

So much, so very much, depends on it.

Flight

There they were . . . thirty or forty geese, slowly walking in their ambling way, pecking at the ground, holding a sort of meditative space . . . on an airport runway. This is the runway I see every morning as I drive on my morning commute. It was an ironic sight. Just as a huge airplane came over my car on its way to landing, the geese rose *en mass* into the air and out of harm's way. But for just a moment there was the mirror image of flight . . . geese to plane . . . plane to geese.

Surely it was out of this vision of flight that the Wright brothers and like-minded adventurers began to dream of human flight. We are fascinated by flight . . . being able to take off from our attachment to earth and to float on the air around us. Most super heroes and heroines have the gift of flight . . . that ability to rise above whatever is happening and to fly away, to float gently on the invisible, to save whatever needs to be saved.

One of my favorite parts of the stories of King Arthur is when Merlin teaches the young Arthur about what it means to be a leader, a king. Merlin, with his magical abilities, turns Arthur into an eagle and sends him off to view the world. When Arthur returns, Merlin asks him what he noticed, what he had learned by being able to fly. Arthur simply says, "There are no boundaries." He goes on to describe how in flying over the land he realized how all the fences, the gates, the walls we erect are really artificial . . . that when viewed from flight the earth is all one, unified.

I am not sure that we have learned this lesson very well. Our sense of unity on this planet gets pulled in countless directions each day. We continue to build barriers, both real and invisible, in an effort to divide, to create some false sense of safety, to keep those unlike us out, to keep those most like us, within.

Oh, to be like the geese, to fly over the land and see not barriers but beauty, not walls but wonder. Perhaps our fascination with flight is not just about being able to get someplace faster, to go to places far away. Perhaps someplace deep inside of us, we also long to be able to have the perspective that allows us to see past the artificial boundaries to what is true . . . a beautiful, resplendent unity.

> *I know all the birds of the air, and all that moves in the field is mine. Those who bring thanksgiving honor me, to those who go the right way, I will show the wholeness of God.* —Psalm 50

Captured

The woman was on her knees in the wet grass, camera poised a few inches away from a few newly fallen leaves. Their red and orange was brilliant against the summer's green, and she knelt to preserve the memory of their colors. I only saw her for a moment as I turned a corner on my way to the office. I really wanted to stop the car and join her, kneeling to honor the ending of one season and the arrival of still another. But I was running late and a car was rushing up behind me, so I kept on, propelled by speed and the urgency of the clock. Inside me, however, I knew she was doing the more noble thing . . . trying to capture the beauty of a fallen leaf . . . a beauty that lasts so briefly.

One of my favorite memories of childhood is collecting leaves, mostly maple or oak, and placing them between pieces of waxed paper. I would arrange them in different configurations, matching and contrasting colors . . . bright yellow, burnt orange, fiery red. Then, with my mother's help, I would gently iron the two pieces of paper together. It was primitive laminating! Then we would hang the paper in the windows, creating a sense of forever falling leaves.

Somehow when I did this I hoped to capture the beauty of the fall colors and hold them forever. But, of course, as the sun shone through the window the leaves still turned brown, dying not on the ground but between the pieces of human-created waxy paper. It is their nature, one that cannot be captured but only gratefully appreciated. The miraculous cycle of birth, life, death, and rebirth could not be contained. It was an important lesson to learn, one each of us, I believe, continues learning with the arrival and departure of the seasons. It is a lesson that keeps us humble and, if we allow ourselves, filled with gratitude.

The autumn season has only begun. There is much time to observe, honor, and be present in the change that is happening around us. Can we capture the beauty and hold it forever? Probably not. But we can kneel down and gives thanks. We can marvel at the ability of unseen forces to take green and turn it into red, yellow, gold, orange. And perhaps, that is our real work.

> *The angel showed me the river of the water of life, bright as crystal ,flowing from the throne of God through the middle of the city. On either side of the river is the tree of life . . . and the leaves of the tree are for the healing of the nations.* —Revelation 22:1-2

Sumac

The fields in our neighborhood and along the roads are showing a brilliant red these days. The color is not coming from the taller trees but from the sumac bushes that have grown wild, planted there by the generosity of birds. During the summer months you don't notice the bushes so much, but as the season begins to turn their brilliance is breathtaking.

The sumac bush has clumps of red berries which provide a wonderful contrast in summer to their deep green leaves. As you walk through the fields, the plant is common, as is its dangerous cousin, poison-ivy. Over the weekend when I noticed the plethora of bushes along the highway, I was reminded of a very significant memory which included sumac.

While directing a children's camp one summer at a church retreat center, the children were working with a fabric artist, learning how to take the gifts of nature and create dyes for yarn and cloth. The theme of the camp was "Bibletimes 29 A.D.," and our goal was to experience some of the crafts, foods, games, and work habits of the early Christians. The fabric artist walked through the woods pointing out different plants that, when boiled, created dyes for otherwise bland clothing.

She pointed out the sumac with its deep scarlet berries and harvested some for our first-century fashions. Placing the brilliant berries in the pot that boiled over the fire, many of the children dreamed of the great red togas they would be wearing later. But as the berries began to boil, the water turned not red, but a rich, beautiful gold. Amazing!

As I saw the sumac, I thought about all the times when our expectation of what something—or someone—has to offer turns out to be completely different. That summer our expectation was that because the berries of the sumac were red, our dye would be red. But the sumac held a surprise . . . gold. How often our expectations allow us only to see the surface of what a colleague, a challenge, a child holds deep within! We see red . . . they carry gold. They are waiting to be warmed enough to offer their inner truest colors.

Don't you think just knowing that the world holds such hidden promise should keep us on our toes, with eyes wide open, watching for the next surprise. What will it be?

The most beautiful thing we can experience is the mysterious.
—Albert Einstein

PART TWO

Road Travels

Stand at the crossroads and look;
ask for the ancient paths,
ask where the good way is, and walk in it,
and you will find rest for your souls.

Jeremiah 6:16

The roads we travel shape us and influence how we see our fellow travelers and how we envision the world. For those of us who seek to understand our lives through a spiritual lens, the roads we travel also help create our image of God. One of my seminary professors once said there is a great similarity between real estate and theology: It's all about "location, location, location." How we see the Holy is filtered through our lens of the world, the place in which we live daily, and the roads we may or may not have the privilege to travel.

A survey in 2005 found that the average American driver spends 24.3 minutes daily driving to work. This adds up to more than 100 hours a year, according to the U.S. Census Bureau's American Community Survey. Think about it: That's more than two weeks of vacation at forty hours per week. Twenty-four minutes is right on target for my one-way commute, so when I read those statistics I was startled. My daily journey of forty-eight minutes, when taken with intention and attention, often provides moments of connection with Spirit. On my daily commutes I have found there are often little guideposts that wake me up and cause me to pause in the mindless activity of a common route. These little wake-up calls come in the form of bumper stickers, road signs, billboards, or simply other people in their cars doing odd or interesting things.

I have a friend who is a spiritual director who prays a breath prayer at stoplights. On his commute he never listens to the radio but instead uses the drive time as prayer time. At a stoplight while he sits in his car waiting for the light to change, he prays: (breath in) "Holy One . . . (breathe out) . . . walk with me this day." I tryed this for a while, but I found I was too focused on the breathing and the praying, and soon the horns were honking for me to get going. So instead I simply keep my eyes and heart open to what might cross my path. If we truly believe God is everywhere, in all things, at all times, then why not accompanying us on our daily drive? Many of these reflections were written when the Spirit brushed by me at fifty-five miles per hour.

Still others were written as I traveled to other places around the country on vacation or retreat. I have found that the gift of a time away from the familiarity of home can open my heart to new experiences and images of the Divine. Being in another location helps me to understand the world view and theological perspectives of others, increasing my acceptance and commitment to the gifts of diversity for the whole people of God.

The prophet Jeremiah's invitation is to stand at the crossroads, looking for the good paths that have brought us this far. With the rising of each day we begin the walk again, looking for what is good and a place to rest our weary souls.

Between Expeditions

I heard Ann Bancroft, Arctic explorer and educator, being interviewed on the radio. After the introduction that included her many accomplishments, the host asked her what she was doing these days. Her reply? "I'm between expeditions right now. Not, "I am not doing anything." or "I don't know what's next for me." But, "I'm between expeditions right now." What a wonderful answer!

Hearing her words I wondered what might happen if we treated all those times when we don't know what the next step will be for us as simply a time "between expeditions." When we are between expeditions, it is easier to be creative in our thought process. We use our imaginations and live by our dreams. We make our questions big and bold in the asking. We spend time mulling over the possibilities rather than limiting the next step with practicalities. We rely on the Spirit's movement to nudge us, to breathe life into the small spaces of our plans. We consult maps and look at all the outlying areas in addition to the well-defined, clear, and familiar roadways.

Are you between expeditions right now? Sometimes this inbetween time is a situation not of our own choosing. If this state of being is brought on through illness, life changes, job loss, grief, depression, we can find ourselves in the land of inbetween. It does not feel like a gift or luxury, but a sentence to be lived out. Other times we have intentionally chosen to leave one place and have no idea where the road will take us. Like the pilgrims of most faith traditions, we are stepping out on a path to which we are prepared to offer our lives. Whatever has led to where we are, I believe there is a gift in thinking of the present moment as ripe with possibility.

In the book of Exodus, the people are always on one expedition or another. From slavery to freedom, from despair to hope, from faithfulness to disobedience . . . on the one hand believing God is with them and the next moment feeling that they have been abandoned completely. Their wilderness is both actual landscape and spiritual exploration. But as Moses led them from one expedition to the next, "God went in from of them in a pillar of cloud by day, to lead them along the way, and in a pillar of fire by night, to give them light, so that they might travel by day and by night. Neither the pillar of cloud by day or the pillar of fire by night left its place in front of the people."

I believe it is the same with us . . . the Holy travels with us even when we are between expeditions.

Home Land

Then God said, "I have observed the misery of my people who are in Egypt; I have heard their cry on account of their taskmasters. Indeed, I know their sufferings, and I have come down to deliver them from the Egyptians, and to bring them up out of that land to a good and broad land, a land flowing with milk and honey."

—Exodus 3:7-8a

A land flowing with milk and honey . . . what a wonderful image . . . an earthly place that is filled with what will sustain, bring joy, feed the spirit. I believe each person has within them that place, that memory of landscape, perhaps the place they were born or the place of their ancestors. This land is the place where their soul rests and finds recognition in the soil that fed their bloodline. It is the place that is in their DNA whether they are aware of it or not. We are, after all, earthbound beings, and this is our home.

I sat and listened to a woman named Dorothy who told us about her people, the Gullah people. These people are the direct descendants of the slaves brought to our country who now reside in the island areas of South Carolina. They have worked hard over the years to maintain their identity, culture, language, music, food, and to keep their ties to the land that was forced upon them. In the course of her storytelling, she explained to us how the people had built their cemeteries on the shore, near the water, because they believed that when they died and were buried, their spirits would be able to cross back over the water and go home again to Africa. I was mesmerized by this idea, by her story, by this deep longing for the land of her ancestors. Now with development, Dorothy told us, and some complicated land ownership laws, these cemeteries are being removed to make way for beach houses and other buildings to support the local economy. How will their spirits find home again?

The scriptures are filled with stories of people who are displaced, in exile, enslaved, who are trying to make their way home. It is one of our common human stories even when we are unaware of it. We each carry the cell memory of our ancestors deep within us that calls us to prefer mountains over water, prairie over desert, the sand over stone. Some people have spent their lives searching for "something" that is just outside their reach, only to arrive in a place they have never been before and feel completed.

Where is your land of milk and honey? Where does your spirit find its home? The poet John Soos writes: "To be of the Earth is to know...the restlessness of being a seed, the darkness of being planted, the struggle toward the light, the pain of growth into the light, the joy of bursting and bearing fruit, the love of being food for someone, the scattering of your seeds, the decay of the seasons, the mystery of death, and the miracle of birth."

No matter the soil of our home, this is the miracle of who we are.

Chaos?

As I was inching along in the line of cars to get on a highway, my eyes fell on a curious bumper sticker. It read: **Chaos—Panic—Fear: My work here is done.** I was startled. What could this mean? What was the intention of the creator? What was the intention of the person who cavalierly pasted this message on their bumper? On the one hand I wanted to laugh, but then the words began to disturb me.

Chaos—Panic—Fear. Who would declare this as their work? Probably each of us could name a few people whose work we believe does just that . . . creates chaos. Sometimes this production of chaos is intentional. Sometimes it is simply because their life situation carries with it energy that moves into our midst, and before we know it we are sucked into their chaotic vortex. Chaos often has panic as its by-product, and where panic lives fear finds a home and takes root. My prayer is that I may never create this negative spiral, though no doubt at times I have.

I would like to of speak for another way of living in and with chaos. Webster defines chaos as:"The disorder of formless matter and infinite space, supposed to have existed before the ordered universe; the state of order existing within apparent disorder, as in the irregularities of a coastline or snowflake." If approached with openness and a hopeful heart, chaos can be the biggest catalyst for creativity. When faced with the chaos of a situation, relationship, project, if we open our eyes to the possibilities within the chaos, creativity moves in and great things can come out of it . . . things as amazing as snowflakes.

Perhaps parts of your life, your work, may seem like they are in chaos right now. Disorder reigns. How different would the work be if this disorder was seen, not as a reason to panic and be fearful, but instead as an opportunity for great dreaming, re-imagining, and creativity? This choice is not always the easy one. We live in a culture that promotes panic and fear at every turn. But the choice for dreamful opportunity is, in my experience, always the rewarding one.

As I read the scriptures and other wisdom writings, it seems to me that all great forward motion has been founded on a creativity that rose out of and above chaos to ask the question, "What is the greatest good that can be done here?" And out of that asking, change, order, and hope are born.

So let me propose another bumper sticker: *Chaos—Creativity—Hope: My Work Here Has Just Begun.*

Anyone out there willing to slap that message on their bumper? Anyone willing to put these words . . . with glue that promises to be very difficult to remove . . . on their car and drive out into the world? I hope so.

Wrap yourselves in the blanket of creativity and see what comes of it. Stay warm and dream.

> *Earth was a soup of nothingness, a bottomless emptiness, an*
> *inky blackness. God's Spirit brooded above the watery abyss. God*
> *spoke: Light! and light appeared. God saw that light was good.*
> —Genesis 1 from *The Message*

Impossible?

*Alice laughed: "There's no use trying," she said; "one can't
believe impossible things."*

*"I daresay you haven't had much practice," said the Queen.
"When I was younger, I always did it for half an hour a day.
Why, sometimes I've believed as many as six impossible things
before breakfast."* —Alice in Wonderland

Impossible. This is a fabulous quote from this wild and crazy story
of Alice and her adventures in Wonderland. I love entertaining impossible ideas. Do you? What can it mean to allow our minds to travel to
the place of "impossible possibility"? Alice's story is one of those rare
gifts, being both for children and for adults. While following Alice's
antics and discoveries, we see the nuggets of wisdom tucked into this
often very convoluted story. Children hear the story from one perspective and are affirmed. Adults read the story and can be challenged to
remember what it was like to be open to the adventure of the impossible.

While most of us don't encounter rabbits that talk or get to dance
with the Queen of Hearts, we often face some pretty challenging
situations that call us to harbor impossible ideas. As we sit down to
hammer out a new plan in our work or try to make sense of a difficult relationship, the gift of impossible thinking can be quite helpful.
When funds are short and there need to be cuts to a budget, impossible thinking can open the door to Wonderland. When we set a goal
to accomplish something that seems important and big in our lives, it
is important to hold on to the idea of being able to achieve the impossible.

I think of all the things that have been impossible ideas in my
lifetime . . . people walking on the moon . . . phones without cords . . .
the internet . . . cures and vaccines for countless diseases . . . collecting
the wind to create power . . . cooking food without fire . . . the list goes
on and on. I can't even imagine all the "impossible" things those who
have lived into their nineties or have reached the age of one hundred
have seen. The gift of imagining what the impossible possibilities will
be for our children and grandchildren is quite thrilling.

How many impossible things can you imagine in this moment?
What might our lives be like if we, like the Queen, spent a half-hour
each day imagining impossible things? Impossible thinking is, I
believe, faith thinking. Impossible thinking is creative thinking. Impos-

sible thinking is Spirit-filled thinking, thinking that gets picked up and blown around by a Spirit that "blows where it will."

There are many needs within our world that may only be solved by impossible thinking. Poverty, homelessness, peace . . . to name only three. Perhaps today is the day to begin embracing the impossible possibilities that will shape the future. Only God knows where it will lead, but I think it is well worth a try. How about you?

Well at World's End

Those who in youth and childhood wander alone in woods and wild places, ever after carry in their hearts a secret well of quietness
—W.B. Yeats

The powers that be, I believe, are conspiring to remind me that I am taking myself too seriously these days. They are putting little hints in my path . . . little bits of words here and there . . . so I will get the message: Lighten up. Play more. Remember the joys of your childhood. It seems no matter what I pick up to read, there is some overt message about letting go of the seriousness of life and finding what in fairy tales is often referred to by Celtic writer Caitlin Matthews as the "well at world's end." It is the place where one comes after searching, working, being tricked by this creature or another, until we arrive by drawing on our deep instinct, finally drinking from the pure waters. Refreshed.

I am reminded of the times that I have observed my own children or another's children playing. With freedom they moved with from swing to swing, from wall to tree, running, jumping, full of the freedom of sheer play. Imagination took them from superhero to warrior, from circus performer to animal, endlessly moving from one playful moment to the next. There was never the sense that anything was impossible to become. I want to remember how to be that way.

A few months ago, I talked with a mother whose son ran up and down our church hallways. Jeans and T-shirt were accessorized by—what else?—a cape. As this young child moved through his play he was both boy and so much more. Who knew when he might be called upon to save the world? As the mom and I talked, I told her how I'd like to keep a cape in my office. On days when I felt I needed a little "something more" to get the job done, I'd wear my cape. I'd put it on and walk about the office, solving this problem and the next with the toss of my cape. My office friends would see me coming and breathe a sigh of relief. I could also keep it in a special place, easily accessible, for my colleagues to borrow when they, too, needed a little more power to deal with what needed to be done.

Those tricks of our childhood run deep within us and are told over and over again in the stories we cherish and tell our children and our grandchildren. Dragons can be slain, trolls that hide under bridges cannot harm us because we know the secret word. Nourishing wells can be found at the end of a dangerous journey, a journey we have used our wits and courage to complete. Normal people embody stories of heroes and heroines, stories of hope and triumph, stories that hold happy endings.

As for me, all I need now is a really cool cape. . . .

If

Earth is a Paradise, the only one we will ever know. We realize it the moment we open our eyes. We don't have to make it a Paradise—it is one. We have only to make ourselves fit to inhabit it.
                                                    —Henry Miller

If you awake early in the morning and are able to take in the day at its birth, you will see it: this Paradise, waking up, or our human eyes and senses awakening to it. This morning I had reason not only to wake early which is my usual pattern, but also to actually walk out into the day. I should preface this by saying that, in general, most Minnesotans are crabby during the winter. I well recall standing at a soccer game during which I experienced snow, rain, brilliant sunshine, and gloomy gray skies . . . all in the period of ninety minutes. This on-going hostage situation of winter makes everyone a little testy.

So this morning as I traveled across the bridge which spans the Minnesota River as it meets up with the Mississippi, I didn't expect to be dazzled. And yet, there it was. On one side of me the half moon stood watch in the blue sky of morning. In my rear view mirror I could see an orangish-pink begin to color the misty horizon. I found myself suspended in the halo of these beacons of night and day. Later as I crossed the bridge back toward the east, the sun was showing itself . . . a bright red ball of fire screaming, "Here I am! Don't miss me!" My eyes were momentarily drawn away from its brilliance to the sight of at least a dozen wild turkeys, huge and glistening in an oily greenish blue, strutting their stuff on the side of a hill. All this before 6:30 a.m.!

And so here I was, someone who just yesterday had said, "To heck with you!" at what seems like a god-forsaken land of never-ending gloomy weather. I had essentially "broken up" with this land. Then this morning I was seduced once again by the remarkable beauty, the unmistakable wonder, the never-ending allure, of this world. This Paradise had once again shown up at my door with a bouquet of flowers, fluttering its eyes, flirting with me. I shrugged my shoulders and said, "O.K., you're right. I love you." And we made up.

If you wake early, that's what can happen. It might work the same if you stay up late and take in the seduction of the descending nighttime. But the Sun does have a way of turning your head . . . and making you fall in love all over again.

Do I not fill heaven and earth? says God. —Jeremiah 23:24

Almost, Not Quite

The last few days have been in the place of "almost but not quite." Driving across the rivers as I do so many times during a day, the trees are putting forth not quite green and not quite yellow as they work to produce their fullness. Walking through my garden, the hostas have pushed their way through the ground, long spiky shoots make circles of what, in just a few weeks, will be fully formed, lush leaves. Other ground cover has peeked through the soil and is beginning to inch out, ready to spread in its usual way, creeping around all in its path.

Of course the tulips have had a head start. They have been slumbering in the dark, cold ground and now stand in their fullness, showing off their colors while their botanical siblings are stretching to become themselves. The crab apple trees outside my office window are trying so desperately to be hot pink . . . and soon they will be. In the next few days the branches will be heavy with shades of red, pink, and fuchsia, waving gently in the spring breezes, sending their sweet scent into the wind. It is a glorious sight.

It is a time of year when one can become so acutely aware of what it means to be alive, to be a part of something much bigger than our human-ness, to literally watch the world come into its fullness. It is the time of year that begs us to become children again, stopping at each interesting thing to see. This brilliant bud . . . this lovely leaf . . . this mossy mound. Why, it could take hours to walk one block!

The "almost but not quite" part of spring invites us to Pay Attention . . . with a capital P and A. If we don't we will miss its unfolding, and that would be a terrible shame, wouldn't it? Because we all know that it doesn't last long, and its gentle beauty is meant to remind us of who we are . . . the ones with words, the ones given to experiencing awe, the ones who can proclaim their praise. We have important work to do, and now is the moment.

Go ahead . . . get out there . . . do what needs to be done!

Embers

The Lord went in front of them in a pillar of cloud by day, to lead them along the way, and in a pillar of fire by night, to give them light, so that they might travel by day and by night.
—Exodus 13.21

The magazines to which I subscribe are mostly filled with pictures. My reading time is devoted to books and newspapers, but I enjoy the luxury of sitting down with a nice cup of tea and mulling over photos in a magazine. Yesterday I opened a copy of *National Geographic Traveler*. It is filled with lots of great places to dream about, to enter into, to spend time with, as a way of taking a small vacation from the ordinary day.

This issue included a special feature on Appalachia. I looked at the beautiful photographs one expects from *National Geographic* and allowed myself the pleasure of reading one of the articles about the Appalachian Valley, a place I know well. I was reminded of something I knew about this area of the country that has always held great meaning to me: Writing about the Tennessee Valley Authority's damming of the rivers in the 1930 s in order to create electricity for the people of these mountains, James Conway tells of the many people who were displaced by the construction and flooding. Those people who had lived in the same place since their ancestors came to this country from Scotland, Wales, England, and Germany had kept the original embers of the fire that had glowed in their hearth from the first days. These embers were the center of the fires that warmed their homes decades later. When they were forced out or willingly left, many carried the embers of that fire to the next place they would live. They might have left their original home, but they carried the fire of their ancestors with them to begin their new life on different soil.

It is a fascinating and comforting image for me. It is also a great metaphor for the fire we all carry with us each day. Many of us carry the fire of ancestors, grandparents and great-grandparents, who continued to tell us the stories of those who sacrificed much so we can now live in the ways we do. Others carry the fire of their faith with them, warming and continuing to uphold them on their life's journey. Still others carry a fire of challenge given to them by those they may never have met but whose very lives have etched their thumbprint on hearts now beating for justice.

Reading this article caused me once again to reflect upon the embers of my home fire and those who carried them through time, from home to home, from heart to heart. I pray I will always have the courage to fan that flame and keep that fire alive to pass on to my children and my children's children.

What embers do you carry with you? What fire is at the center of your life that warms the core of who you are? How does that fire get passed from place to place, from person to person? In this time of changing seasons, it is something to consider to continue the work of carrying the fire forward into the future.

> *Thank you, Father, for your free gift of fire. Because it is through fire that you draw near to us every day. It is with fire that you constantly bless us. Bless this fire today. Make this fire a worthy thing. Let it become a reminder of your love, a reminder of life without end.*
>   —*Masai prayer*

New Things

I took a road trip from Minnesota to northern Illinois. Driving through Wisconsin, the words of the prophet Isaiah kept running through my mind: :*I am about to do a new thing, now it springs forth, do you not perceive it?"* Really, those words actually ran through my mind several times as I looked out the car window at the landscape along the freeway. Those words written long ago reflect the writer's experience of exile and the hope for the restoration of the people of Israel. But for me, gazing out the window, the words also spoke to the visible rebirth of creation around us.

The land stood, gray, brown, sometimes tinged gold; the outlines of corn and soybean fields looked like a well-worn patchwork quilt. They seemed poised, just on the edge of bringing forth something new. The birch trees, now even more brilliantly white against greening grass, reached toward the heavens with red-tipped branches ripe with leaves longing to be green. Wild turkeys roamed the fields pecking at whatever food they could find, leftovers from a long, hard winter. And young deer could be seen moving slowly across the fields, becoming statues at the change in a traffic pattern, hoping to ensure their safety by the sheer will of their stillness.

Overhead, flocks of geese and other birds flew north, possibly peering down on the few patches of snow left in places where the sun had not penetrated. Looking out my car window at seventy miles per hour, I saw a mother cow licking the body of a newly born calf. Newness . . . springing forth everywhere.

Of course, newness springs forth around us all the time, but it is never quite so brilliant as in these early days of a much anticipated spring. During these days I am always so aware of the Sacred . . . how small I am in the larger scheme of things . . . how beautiful and wonderful it is to be alive . . . the gifts all around us.

I have a favorite greeting card taped to my office door. The artist does odd little drawings of colorful geometric people, this one accompanied by the words: "Everyday she cried at least once because the world is so beautiful and life is so short."

Newness, beauty, promise, hope . . . do you not perceive it?

Delight

I heard a story on public radio about a poet named Sally Crabtree who lives in England. Sally was hired by the National Rail Service to soothe the tempers of those who must wait for sometimes tardy trains. Her work is to show up on a train platform, set up what is called a poet-tree—a metal tree that has various and sundry items hanging from it—and invite bystanders to choose something. She then proceeds to entertain those waiting for the train by creating an impromptu poem about that item. She will also create a poem about a person standing nearby or whatever else strikes her fancy at the moment. It is difficult to imagine something happening like this in the U.S., especially on purpose. It seems even more unlikely to be done at the direction of big business, to somehow make the patron feel better while at the same time perhaps being inconvenienced. "The purpose of poetry is to delight," says Crabtree.

I loved that statement, and I loved the idea that someplace, someone is being employed to "delight." What a glorious goal for one's work! How might our work be done if at least one of our goals was to delight—to delight those who walk into our office, our store, our restaurant, our home, our church? "Allow me, if you would, to delight you with this proposal." "Please, try this soup. . . . I hope you find it delightful". "Welcome to worship today. May you find something that lifts your soul and delights your life." You get the picture.

Crabtree's notion about poetry's purpose is correct, I believe. But I also think poetry draws people in because it is a minimalist art form. In a world that throws more words at us that we can take in, where talk radio and talk television shows drone on and on about a single, often trivial subject for numbing hours, to come face to face with a few words that express our deepest feelings seems like a life preserver tossed to a drowning society.

So, today, I hope to be a person of few words . . . but well chosen ones . . . words that might perhaps bring delight to someone who needs them most.

> *Enough. These few words are enough. If not these words, this breath. If not this breath, this sitting here. This opening to the life we have refused again and again until now. Until now.*
> —David Whyte

Answers

I followed a green minivan with a license plate that simply read "ANSWERS." It seemed to me a very bold statement to display on your car. Since I was following it for quite some time, I began to imagine what kind of answers the owner of this car might possess. Was the driver a palm reader, fortune teller, a reader of tea leaves? Was the car being driven by a mathematician or scientist or maybe a Sudoku enthusiast? Or perhaps the person behind the wheel was a religious professional of some sort—like me—one who was certainly clearer about what they *know* than I am. Whatever the answers this person claims to have must be important . . . important enough to pay the extra cash for specialized license plates.

Are you a person more comfortable with answers or with questions? I've always been more a "question" person myself. I love questions. I love entering into the ebb and flow of questions, the process of thinking through all the possibilities that a questions poses. For me, questions and mystery go hand in hand, and most often I find the sacred within the mystery.

One of my favorite quotes, which I come back to time and time again comes from Rainer Maria Rilke's *Letters to a Young Poet*. "Be patient toward all that is unresolved in your heart. . . . Try to love the questions themselves. . . . Do not now seek the answers, which cannot be given because you would not be able to live them—and the point is to live everything. Live the questions now. Perhaps you will then gradually, without noticing it, live along some distant day into the answers."

These words always remind me of the times I have tried to force the answers to the questions I am carrying . . . trying to make answers fit, rather than relaxing into the search, allowing a deeper truth to flow out of the Mystery. All the energy, the struggling, the pushing and pulling, trying to beat the answer out of the question, so I can "get on with my life" Rather than just holding the question gently, trusting Spirit to walk with me into some greater experience of understanding, some deeper knowledge, I end up frustrated and exhausted with my own impatience.

Answers? Questions? Questions? Answers? The point, after all, is to live everything.

> *For now we see in a mirror, dimly, but then we will see face to face. Now I know only in part; then I will know fully, even as I have been fully known.* —1 Corinthians 13:12

Outstanding

Traveling the highways through Wisconsin, Illinois, Indiana, and into Ohio, I have become aware of the fields that bookend my drive. On each side of the road stands acre after acre of corn and soybeans. I was reminded of the greeting card that offers the words: "Congratulations! You are outstanding in your field." The image is usually a field with one person standing alone in a field of identical items. Those items change depending on the intention of the card.

On this drive, I witnessed field after field of corn. Now I know nothing about corn . . . its growing patterns, its different types. But what I observed is that certain fields had red tassels and other fields had golden tassels. Driving along it was like moving through a chorus line of tall redheads on one side and equally as tall blondes on the other. I imagined them in a kick line of dance, Rockettes-style, competing across the asphalt divide as the drivers in the cars made up the revolving audience.

Sprinkled among the corn was, of course, soybeans. Shorter, brilliant green, they seemed to pale in their dramatic impact on the horizon. Every now and then, however, a stray corn seed had flown through the air and planted itself among the soybeans. Without the benefit of cross-pollination (I do know this much), they had not grown to maturity, but they were certainly taller than the field of short green soybeans in which they stood. They were truly . . . outstanding.

And then at one point my son said: "Look, Mom. Sunflowers!" It was true. There they were, breaking up the pattern. The queen of flowers standing in all their marvelous beauty facing the rays of the sun. An entire field of yellow ecstasy. Outstanding!

At some place along the road in Indiana, a moving truck had lost a part of its cargo. A rocking chair sat quietly beside the road, flanked by redheads on one side and blondes on the other. It looked like a good spot to observe the dance of late summer. If someone had been sitting there witnessing it all, I don't think I would have been surprised. It seemed like the right thing to do. Outstanding!

Bent Backs

And Ruth the Moabite said to Naomi, 'Let me go to the field and glean among the ears of grain, behind someone in whose sight I may find favor.' So she went. She came and gleaned in the field behind the reapers. Boaz said to the reapers, "God be with you." They answered, "God bless you." —from Ruth 2

I began my morning as many laborers do. I rose early and put on clothes I don't care much about. I loaded my car with boxes, filled my coffee cup, and headed to the field . . . to pick strawberries. It was a beautiful summer morning, not too hot, not too "buggy." Arriving at the field, I found myself surrounded by would-be farmers of all ages. Small children moved slowly, accompanied by parents or grandparents who guided them in their picking. Men and women picked side by side. Those who owned the farm moved among the pickers, exchanging pleasantries with the workers. Each of us were picking these berries for the joy of it, for the experience of harvesting a bit of our own food, for the glory of the morning, and because we could. We each left the field with the ripe, red berries scenting our cars with their sweetness and staining our fingertips with their color. Whether we made the realization or not, we were a privileged people . . . privileged to have the ability and means to pick these summertime specialties . . . privileged to pick what we want for as long or as short a time as we wanted.

As I drove away from the field, my eyes fell back upon the rows of green where the juiciness of summer lay hidden under leaves. The sun was beginning to warm the patches, and I could see the heat reflecting off the ground. Within a few hours the experience of picking these luscious berries would not be nearly as pleasant, the pickers not nearly as comfortable. Across the field, dotting the landscape, were the bent backs of the workers.

And then I thought of all the bent backs that bring food to our tables . . . the workers who fill the fields across this land, gleaning and harvesting fruits and vegetables, many for wages that are lower than what many of us would consider acceptable. These workers are not people who are privileged to "play" farmer as I had. These are the ones who bend their backs to pick the berries I eat in the cold of a Minnesota January. These are the ones who kneel in the dirt and soil for long hours while their children work beside them or sleep in the shade nearby. These are the workers who toil in the fields because it provides a life and livelihood for their families.

For me, this morning was a gift. I knelt and picked fruit I did not plant or tend. I give thanks for those who brought the strawberries this far and for the privilege of picking them. At the same time, I pay homage to all those who day after day bend their backs to feed this nation, this world. Blessings be upon you.

Oversize Load

Traveling across the interstate highway system, I have been surrounded by semi-trailer trucks carrying any variety of cargo. There were the usual trucks carrying smaller trucks and cars on their way to dealerships. There were those with half of a trailer home . . . followed a mile or so later by the matching other half. There were trucks carrying large signature yellow and green John Deere farm equipment and those carrying other even larger earth movers in the traditional screaming shade of yellow. One truck carried several small military Humvees, painted only a dull, light brown, waiting, I guessed, for the rest of their camouflage to be added at another location. What they shared in common was the large, bright yellow signs declaring, "Oversize Load." As if this wasn't completely obvious!

The most interesting and surprising were the trucks that carried the grain silos, tipped horizontally . . . shining silver bullets, zooming at seventy miles per hour down the open road. The irony of them moving at such a speed through all the corn and soybean fields made me laugh. Their sisters and brothers, all grounded and fully vertical, watched their movement from the farms nearby.

In addition to the large sign which read "Oversize Load," each truck was decorated with flashing yellow and red lights. Red flags jutted out from the cargo, waving frantically in the freeway wind. The silos, in particular, were accompanied by smaller Jeeps, one leading the way, another bringing up the rear, lights flashing. They seemed so small and helpless as heralds of these large, silver cylinders, like tugboats for the road.

"Oversize Load" . . . I think of all the people I know who are carrying their own oversize loads, life cargo that seems more than reasonable. Friends who are dealing with illness and uncertainty. Still others who are heavy with worry over children and grandchildren. There are those who shoulder the responsibility of aging parents, difficult jobs, dwindling resources. Teenagers and young adults walking into a world that throws so much, often too much, at them at one time.

At times like this, wouldn't it be great if these people were surrounded by flashing lights and signs saying, "Oversize Load. Be gentle and kind with me today"? Wouldn't it be wonderful if there were smaller vehicles leading the way and following to protect and keep them safe from everything else on the road? Wouldn't it be helpful if those around needed to slow down a bit and become more aware of all that others were carrying?

Given the fact that we can't decorate ourselves with flashing or warning signs, maybe the best I can do today is to be aware . . . of the eyes of those I meet, the way shoulders are rounded or slumped, the tone of voices, the energy projected . . . and remember that some might be carrying an oversize load. I'll try to give enough space, perhaps even a little protection, say a prayer, be kind, generous, and careful. Hopefully, it will make the traveling easier, gentler.

Rescue

Piglet sidled up to Pooh from behind.

"Pooh!" he whispered.

"Yes, Piglet?"

"Nothing," said Piglet, taking Pooh's paw. "I just wanted to be sure of you."

—A.A. Milne in *The Many Adventures of Winnie the Pooh*

This is a warning: The following words may be disturbing.

It began as a normal afternoon commute from Minneapolis to St. Paul. At rush hour I never expect much . . . slow going, stop and start traffic, a little time listening to the news of the day on the radio. The temperature was very warm so I expected some stalled vehicles, and I was not disappointed.

While crossing the bridge across the Mississippi, I noticed some strange movement along the outside of a big tractor trailer truck. What was it? I opened my window to allow a little air into the car and got a whiff of, could it be . . . "farm smell"? As my car inched up alongside the truck, there they were . . . tiny piglet snouts poking out of the metal holes in the trailer. I could see the babies moving about, jostling for space. I was at once taken by how cute they were and heartbroken to see them confined in this way. I couldn't stop myself from speaking to them out the window. My car moved past the truck, and we continued our halting dance across town.

Engrossed in listening to a report on the economy, I hadn't really noticed that the truck had moved far ahead of me. I had been distracted by other stalled vehicles and yet another pulled over by the police. A young man was being searched. I sent a silent prayer his way for both he and the officer. Who knows what complications their lives hold?

Soon I was involved in another slow down. This time as my view cleared I could see cars completely stopped. A woman was moving gingerly in the middle of the freeway reaching out toward the hot, black asphalt. There in the middle of the road was a tiny piglet. Somehow it had broken free and pushed its way through the narrow slots of the trailer. How? Suddenly we commuters were suspended in time as this woman, who probably had never held a pig before in her life, reached down and picked up the pale pink, writhing animal. I don't know if it was injured, just stunned from the fall, or rightfully frightened. Holding the piglet and looking around, she seemed to consider her options before gently lifting the squealing creature into her car. I rolled down my window and shouted out my thanks . . . .for her bravery, for her compassion. She looked equally as stunned as the little swine. Logically she must have been wondering, "What do I do with a lost pig?"

It had started out as a normal evening commute. But it became a time of prayer, a touch with adventure, an observance of a grand escape, an act of selfless compassion, and a courageous rescue. Nameless woman, rescuer of pigs: Blessings be upon you wherever you are.

As God's children, holy and beloved, clothe yourselves with compassion, kindness, meekness, and patience. —Colossians 3:12

Graffiti

The freeways in the Twin Cities are wild on some summer mornings. I was trying to make it to the office for an early meeting. As I moved through my usual route, traffic stopped. I drummed my fingers on the steering wheel, began some deep breathing, and settled in for a long wait. I noticed several cars pass on my right, veering off at the next exit. I decided to follow. I was already going to be late; I could be late and at least still be moving.

Passing a lake, I watched runners and walkers crossing over the water that shone brilliant blue in the morning sun. Bicyclists sped by . . . wisdom on wheels on mornings like this. The drive became gift as I traveled through neighborhoods I rarely visit, bungalows nestled on tidy lawns, flower boxes overflowing with the fullness of August blossoms. As I moved on, I drove by run-down houses, lawns rubbed free of grass, with debris littering the sidewalks. A different look at our city.

And then, there is was. An abandoned church. Boarded up rounded, cathedral windows, pale blue paint on the front door, chipped cement steps. And then I saw the words someone had painted on that door: "I hope you live the longest life." This message were scrawled across the lonely, bedraggled door, words of blessing I would have missed had I decided to snake along the freeway.

"I hope you live the longest life" . . . I wonder who painted those words? Who felt compelled to offer such a hopeful blessing along a street that lacks care, one that seems surrounded by trouble and despair? This graffiti artist, paint can in hand, chose to anonymously offer kindness and hope in spite of everything around them. Unlike other graffiti we see along walls or on signs, these words sent a beam of light shining into the street, into the hearts of all who would see.

The prophet Jeremiah, speaking on God's behalf, to a people who walked in exile so long ago wrote: "For surely I know the plans I have for you, plans for your welfare and not for harm, to give you a future with hope."

Somewhere in my city another prophet walks the streets, paint can in hand, offering blessing and hope: "I hope you live the longest life."

Enough to Last

In this day, give us your strength,
Enough to last the day.
In work and play, in rest and sleep,
Enough to last the day.
Supply and feed us in our need.
Give us today our daily bread,
Enough to last the day.
The manna for our bodies, strength,
Enough to last the day.
Supplying, satisfying and full.

—Frances Ballantyne

Have you ever noticed that when you go camping or even on a trip, you take just what you need? No extraneous stuff. Just the necessities. Well, at least most of us do. Our family has always been reminded when we travel of what is really necessary for any given day. There is a wonderful simplicity when you have just a couple of changes of clothing, a sleeping bag, a cup and plate, enough silverware to eat a meal, and a good book for entertainment. Even if you throw into the mix a tent, a flashlight, toothbrush and toothpaste, soap and a towel or two—it adds up to very little.

As Americans we are often shocked at the small refrigerators of people in other countries. Their kitchens are not equipped for amassing of large quantities of produce or frozen foods. Most people around the world buy what they need for a day or two at most. Living this way allows you to connect with the neighborhood grocer, the farmers at the market, your friends down the street. It is a way of living that promotes community and a reminder of the ways our lives are interconnected. I long for that at times.

We traveled this weekend, and I was once again reminded of how little is really necessary for a good day, a really good day. We carried only a little bit of food, clean water, a book for passing the time, comfortable shoes for walking, a few layers of clothes to weather all the changes of season in a day. It really doesn't take much. And yet we often spend so much of our time storing up stuff . . . food, money, resources for a rainy day that may never come. We don't know. It could, but we just don't know.

So this prayer jogged my memory, and my conscience, to remember to ask for only what I need . . . enough to last this day. The scriptures are filled with stories of unwise people who tried to hoard bread or money and ended up with rotting resources. It is a good lesson. The scriptures are also filled with stories of the wise ones who learned what it was like to treasure the gifts of this day, this moment in time, and to be thankful for having enough to last this day.

As for me, I want to follow the ways of the wise ones, savoring the simplicity of what is given for the good of this day. Tomorrow, who knows what will be needed? We'll just have to wait and see.

Equinox

This is my song, O God of all the nations,
a song of peace for lands afar and mine.
This is my home, the country where my heart is;
here are my hopes, my dreams, my holy shrine;
But other hearts in other lands are beating
with hopes and dreams as true and high as mine.

These words written in 1934 by Lloyd Stone reflect the first stanza of a hymn that is a favorite in my faith community. Set to the haunting tune of "Finlandia" by Jean Sibelius, it is the song most often requested by people. It is a beautiful tune, regal and heart moving. While the tune is lovely, I believe it is the words that people want to sing. They want to claim their love for this country, for the area of the country in which they live, and to pay homage to the land that has shaped their view of the world, their understanding of the presence of the Holy.

I think there is also a wonderful sense of humility in the lyrics that we all want to try to embrace. The recognition that our land is so precious to us stirs our hearts. But the recognition that fills us with a deep humbleness is that each human shares the same deep love for their own land.

On one of my favorite radio shows, they often play songs about Lake Superior. I will find my heart tugging in my chest as I listen to the love songs to this Great Lake and think of the times when I have walked its shores and stared out at the expanse of powerful and ancient wisdom that make up its waters. A person who has never experienced this mighty lake would not react in the same way I do, just as I could not feel the same love and affection for, say, a lake in China or any other part of the world. But my belief is that, just as I can be moved to tears by the beauty of this body of water, so others all around the world find that deep meaning in the land that surrounds them, that defines them, that they call home.

Today marks the autumnal equinox in which all over the world for the most part, humans will experience an equal amount of daylight and darkness. Today we will be held in the same amount of sun light and the same amount of night light as those who live in countries with which we are at war. Those fighting in Iraq and Afghanistan will be held today by the sun and the moon just as we are held. Though this is always true, the equinox becomes the great equalizer in some ways. What if we all marked this day by honoring this astronomical similarity rather than focusing on the ways in which we are different? What might happen? How might the world change? How might we change? It is humbling thought.

> *My country's skies are bluer than the ocean,*
> *and sunlight beams on cloverleaf and pine;*
> *but other lands have sunlight too, and clover,*
> *and skies are everywhere as blue as mine.*
> *O hear my song, thou God of all the nations,*
> *a song of peace for their land and for mine.*

As we end our day and say goodbye to the day in which we are all equal in light and darkness, perhaps our prayer might be for those in lands far from ours who love their home as much as we do. And that prayer might begin the peace we long to see.

Feathers

Hope is the thing with feathers
That perches in the soul,
And sings the tune—without the words,
And never stops at all. . . .

—Emily Dickinson

Recently I have had many conversations about hope. Through our worship, our faith community is entering a time of reflection and contemplation on the theme, "Harvest of Hope." Hope. As we have talked, we have tried to differentiate between "hope" and "wish" or "dream." Hope seems somehow deeper, more long-lasting. I can wish for a new car, but hope doesn't seem to fit that kind of desire. Dreams are important and telling, whether awake or asleep, but hope is still something deeper than that.

One person described a particularly difficult time in his life when hope seemed nearly impossible. But through prayer and contemplation, he became acutely aware of the deep kindness that lives at the heart of the universe. That kindness became the well from which hope nourished his despairing soul. Not wishes, but hope.

When I think about 9/11, I am reminded of the visible hope that I experienced the days following that very dark time for our country, for our world. Our house rests in the flight pattern for the airport, so we are accustomed to the sounds of planes going overhead with regularity. Spending time outside in the beautiful fall weather seemed healing in those days. My memory may be colored, but it seemed to me the sun shone particularly bright those days following the tragedy. Though people's hearts were heavy and tears welled in our eyes, the sun seem to warm our pain.

But during these days it wasn't even the sun shining that connected me with the deep sense of hope. It was the geese. You see, during those days our neighborhood was silent . . . no sounds of planes landing or taking off. Just the silence of the open, crystal blue sky. And then the geese would fly over head, honking, rising from the streams and fields that dot our landscape. They would rise majestically into the air headed south, doing what they instinctively knew how to do. I remember thinking, "They don't know." They don't know what's happened. They don't know our sadness. They don't know they are supposed to be grounded, not flying.

But in later days I rethought that statement. Perhaps they did know. They knew that the sun would rise and set and the seasons would change just as they always have, guiding them from north to south and back again. They may even have known that there will be great joy and great tragedy, and that time and life will continue. Perhaps, more than other creatures, they know that hope is "a thing with wings that perches in the soul". . . and never stops at all.

Flowing

Water flows from high in the mountains. Water runs deep in the earth. Miraculously water comes to us, and sustains all life.
—Thich Nhat Hanh

These days I am looking for what sustains. There are so many words flying around in the airwaves, so much rhetoric of hate and mean spiritedness, that I am looking underneath rocks and couch cushions for what it is that can sustain my spirit, my hope. I have been in the presence of those who have been tossed about by the circumstances of the world in ways that has drowned their internal self-respect. It breaks my heart to be present to their stories. I listen to the nightly news and hear words that cut to the depths of our collective hearts. What to do? What to do?

A friend who has one of the kindest hearts I know said that last week he simply needed to go to the river . . . to go to the river and sit and watch its gentle power as it makes its way to the ocean. "All rivers whether they flow east or west, have arisen from the sea and return to the sea." said Meister Eckhart, the medieval mystic. The river flows, always in connection to the place from which it came from and where it will return. For me, there is such kindness and hope in that image. The river flowing out of the sea and back again reminds me of all the ways I am connected to the greater world, and that is an important thing to remember when human words are being carefully crafted to tear us apart and make us believe otherwise.

Each day I have the blessing of crossing the Mississippi River at least two or three times. The concrete and steel that holds me above this mighty body of water can make me feel separate from its waters. But in truth, I am not. Over the next days I, too, want to go to the river even if it is by way of a bridge. I want to remember the deep and spiritual ways I am connected to all that is. I want to hold on tight to that wisdom and not let the voices that screech pull me in other directions. I want to be reminded of what really sustains and drink deeply from it.

Start . . .

*Once upon a time, the ancients tell us, a disciple said to the rabbi,
"God took six days to create the world and it is not perfect. How
is that possible?"*

"Could you have done better?" the rabbi asked.

"Yes, I think I could have," the disciple said.

*"Then what are you waiting for?" the rabbi said. "Go ahead.
Start working."* —A Hasidic tale

Many years ago I came across the writings of Matthew Fox. It was
in his book *Original Blessing* that I came to understand the concept of
co-creation, and it has influenced how I think about my work in the
world ever since. His embrace of the theology of original blessing instead of original sin makes sense to me and has guided how I articulate
my own faith, my own understanding of how God moves in the world,
how I move in the world. The basic gist of his theology is this: We are
all in this business of creating the world . . . God . . . me . . . you . . . all
the time, it never stops.

Now this, of course, was a very different message than the one I
was taught in Sunday school. That message contained a God who created the world . . . *perfect* . . . and we humans messed it up and that is
why things are the way they are. I have to admit that there was something within me that never truly bought that message. When I read
Original Blessing, my life, the church, my faith, my image of God began
to find a deeper grounding—for me, a more authentic grounding.

If I am a co-creator with God in and of the world, that has real
power. If the Holy and I are in this together, what responsibility do I
have to take this work seriously? To do my part?

I've been thinking about this lately because I have found myself
staggering toward cynicism. As I read the papers, listen to political
candidates, hear speeches from church leaders, it is really easy for me
to feel powerless, voiceless. What can I possibly do to end senseless
war? How can I possibly be a voice for justice in our church? What can
I do to stop the destruction of this beautiful, amazing planet?

That's when it hits me. . . . *I am a co-creator*. Little old me . . . with all
my flaws, my insecurities, my doubts, my short-sighted-ness. This is
not a perfect world by a long shot. But it is the world in which the Creator has flung me . . . and you . . . all of us for this time in the history of

the universe. And we are asked simply to do our part . . . however we discern it.

I don't know what a perfect world is. But I do have a notion of what a more-perfect world would look like. And that world does not include tyranny, oppression, hunger, hopelessness, war, injustice. It would include honor for all God's creations . . . and all means ALL.

So, today I will fight against the cynicism that grows with power-lessness. Instead I will remember that we are in this together . . . you . . . me . . . and the One who breathed and loved us into being. And we are ALL counting on one another . . . today, tomorrow, and every day.

Grab Me

Recently I have been at my seminary alumni gathering. It is always wonderful to see people you've known in what sometimes seems like another life, catch up with them, hear the amazing stories of the work they are doing.

On the first day of this gathering, we were able to attend worship in the beautiful new chapel that has been added since most of us were students. It was a worship experience led by current students and was centered around the theme of how, as God's people, we are all a part of a very large puzzle bringing our gifts and sharing them with the world. The words and the music were all lovely, the leaders earnest and fresh in their delivery. The central ritual included coming forward to take a piece of a large world map puzzle that graced the worship table. As gentle music played, people filed forward in the way we all have been trained to do in the church and then labored over the choice of what piece of the world they wanted to take.

Near what we thought was the end of the ritual a voice from the musicians rang out: "Will someone grab me?!" I turned to see three people rush to the side of the violin player, a young man who had played so beautifully the music we had sung. He stood, hands at his side, his head reaching a bit toward the ceiling, a smile pasted across his face. He was blind. He did not want to be left out of ritual at hand, and so he did what was necessary. He called out to be grabbed!

As he grasped the arm of one who had come to his rescue, I thought of all the times in his life when he must have yelled something similar. I also thought of all the times even those of us who are sighted want to . . . need to . . . yell: "Will someone grab me?" How often when life throws a dangerous curve in our road do we long to yell to someone, anyone, "Grab me"? And then there are those times when the work we are doing seems so lonely that we want to know another person is there to walk with us for support or to help us see the way through. Grab me! There have been times in my own life when the situation seemed so unmanageable that I wanted to yell out, "Will someone grab me?" How about you?

As we travel our days, may the path below our feet be solid and sure. And if by chance it isn't, may we have the courage to call out for the help we need. May our words, "Will someone grab me?" be answered by the gentle touch of another, and may we walk together into what is just at the edge of our vision.

Every Day

Imagine once again the goal of your journey. What is your way? How do you see yourself wending your way there? In what way are you walking? As a tourist in search of entertainment? A no-mad adrift? An explorer? In ancient Sanskrit, the word for chess player was the same as that for pilgrim. Try to see yourself on a chess board. What is your next move?   —Phil Cousineau

The mornings have been very dark. And the darkness of night comes earlier than ever. We are in those days when it is not yet winter, but not completely fall, and certainly not summer. Autumn has decided to extend its colorful stay. As I look out of our living room window, the last tree in our yard to lose its leaves every season is showing a brilliant red. I returned from fall in Scotland to the waning days of fall in Min-nesota and feel blessed to have been surrounded every day by orange, yellow, red, and brown . . . the passionate hues of a dying summer.

The rhythm of my days is now filled with meetings, laundry, traf-fic, the stuff of a work-filled life. Gone is the free-form sense of what it means to be on pilgrimage, on holiday. And yet, even as I write those words, I know it is not true. One clear memory I hold is of a circle of fellow travelers. We sat and reflected on what we had experienced during a day of pilgrimage . . . prayer . . . singing . . . Scripture . . . the joy of eating lovely food with equally lovely people . . . some time for writing . . . other time for walking . . . savoring the gifts of fresh air, beautiful landscape, the sacredness of creation. At this point, someone said: "Why do we think we have to board ferries and go to far off lands to have this experience of pilgrimage?" We all fell silent. Why, indeed?

Isn't every day a pilgrimage? That is, if we are intentional about this path we travel with the Holy, isn't every day an opportunity to pray, sing, revel in each blessed bite of food, each precious face we meet? If we are open to the ways of our living, isn't there always time for sacred texts in whatever way we name and claim them? Isn't there always the time for walking and breathing in the gift of the trees to us . . . the oxygen that keeps us alive? And if we really admit it to our-selves, isn't there always at least one moment (or more) when we can take the time to watch the changing of the color, the falling of a leaf, the entrance of yet another season in our life?

Tomorrow will come with all the possibilities of every day. We can choose to see it as another box to cross off on the calendar, as a list of chores to be accomplished. Or tomorrow can be the beginning of a pilgrimage. The pilgrimage we call our life.

Artificial Light

For several days we have been traveling in the islands off the coast of Georgia and South Carolina. We have witnessed amazing wild life, some that are unusual to our Midwestern eyes. We have also witnessed some birds that may spend the summer days in our Minnesota backyard. Seeing them gave new meaning to the term "snowbird."

This Low Country, as it is called, is the home of the loggerhead turtles, those amazing creatures that come ashore to lay their eggs on the beaches surrounded by marshes and salt water. They live a precarious life. Signs in a nature preserve stated: *"Loggerhead turtles find their way to the nest by the light of the moon. No artificial light please!"* I am imagining that in late May and early June many eager tourists line the beaches to see the loggerheads make their way onto the beach. Those same people probably carry flashlights to get a better look at this miraculous phenomenon and could throw the turtles off their natural course.

I thought of the many times I had been thrown off by "artificial" light. Those times when I have been lured by the glow of material possessions, fancy this or that, the fleeting words of recognition and affirmation. Following that artificial light almost always leads away from the internal, natural path. If the loggerheads are thrown off by the artificial light, they will not return to their rightful home. So it is with we humans. If we are too dazzled by the outward light, we ignore our own inward light and lose our way.

Last night we walked the beach and stood looking up at the night sky. On these sandy, damp beaches full of mounds of driftwood and fallen trees, there is very little artificial light from tall buildings or large cities. The constellations, those guiding stars of our ancestors blinked brightly, as they have since the beginning of time. Staring heavenward, the natural lights of our universe told us exactly where we stood in the scheme of things. Without artificial light to throw you off, it is easy to remember who you are and whose you are . . . and the way home.

PART THREE
Traveling Companions

Each Christmas my biological family, my husband and sons, gather what we refer to as our "created" family. This gathering of people that began as a sanctuary for those who live far from family, over the years, has become a true circle of care that behaves like the family most people long to have. We have shared births, deaths, graduations, job loss, illness, and all of life's complexities and joys together.

At some point in the evening celebration, we come together and participate in a ritual that came to us through the Hungarian grandmother of one of those in our circle. She begins by passing out small pieces of wafer called oplakty, imprinted with the image of an angel. We stand, our hands extended as if to receive the sacrament, silent. After all have received she says, "Look around the circle. If you are ever lost in the woods, remember these people, and you will find your way home."

Having a circle of people, a community whose faces you can remember when you are lost in the woods or the world is powerful. In the Christian story, I imagine Jesus knew this power as he began his ministry, gathering those who were fishing or building or planting, to join him on the unfolding of his own spiritual journey. I imagine this same vagabond group of traveling companions held one another in tender care as they embarked on what turned out to be the journey of their lives. As they shared meals, stories, prayer, healing, and transformation, they became the kin-dom of God for one another.

I believe all people, whether part of a faith tradition or not, long for a community in which they are known and valued for their uniqueness, their true selves. The reflections that follow speak to the encounters of community I have had and how in those face-to-face moments the presence of the Sacred became clearer to me. I truly believe it is difficult to have an experience of God outside of community. We all need someone who really knows us and, through their love, compassion, hope, shows us "God with skin on."

Each Sunday in the community in which I am privileged to help lead worship, we invite people to look around at the faces gathered. "Surely we are the presence of God for one another in this moment," we say. In that flash of recognition, surprise, or questioning, something wonderful happens. Heads often turn, seeing the faces they may have glossed over before, and a new kind of glow begins to settle across the community. Like Jacob who encounters God in his ladder-climbing dream, we all come to the same realization, "Surely God is in this place," for we can see that Presence shining back at us.

Hamba nathi mkululu wethu.

Come, walk with us the journey is long.

Traditional South African

Wings

Be like the bird
That, pausing in her flight
Awhile on boughs too slight,
Feels them give way
Beneath her and yet sings,
Knowing that she hath wings.

—Victor Hugo

I have been doing some midwinter decluttering. In a bag of letters I found this poem written on a three-by-five index card. Though the writer's name was not on the card, I knew exactly who had written it and when. At some point during a dark and difficult time in my life, one of the dear saints of our church had tucked this poem into a card or letter she had sent me. I remember receiving several such "love" notes from her during this time. The notes were extremely helpful to me, not only for their beautiful sentiments, but because I knew that they were also accompanied by her prayers. I knew this woman's prayer patterns well and I knew that in the early morning hours she had other index cards placed near her Bible and her comfortable chair. Those cards held the names of people for whom she had been praying for days, weeks, even years. When I would see her, she would often ask me about someone, recounting their illness or difficulties, asking me how things were going for them. A few years ago, when this saint had passed on from this world, I remember feeling that one of the great pray-ers in my life, in the life of our church, was lost to us. I did not know who would take up such a mantle.

This poem holds so many metaphors for our fragile, human lives, doesn't it? Don't we all feel, at times, as if the boughs on which we rest are too slight? I know I certainly do. There are those times when the weight of what we carry threatens to break the very ground on which we stand. When that bough gives way, we often feel as if we are going to fall with a harsh thud. And yet, if we allow ourselves to rest into the assurance of who we truly are, God's beloved ones, we can find the memory of our wings. This praying saint sent me this poem to guide my memory. In finding this card, I am once again held in her wisdom . . . and her encouragement of my own.

If we allow ourselves, we can probably conjure up the names of people who are our "holy reminders." Those people, with a word, a call, a note, a nod, help us to remember the fullness of who we are. These are the people, I believe, who offer us unconditional love, though we may not always define it in that way. These are the people who nearly always see the best in us and, even when they don't, they honor the relationship, not with judgment, but with a knowing glance. Sometimes these people are our parents or siblings. Most often they are people who have decided, for whatever reason, that they are our earth-traveling companions who love us just the way we are. What a gift!

The reciprocity of this kind of relationship is that we offer that same kindness, gentleness, generosity to another. Because we have been given the gift of these people who help us see the sacred nature of our living, we can make that same offering. And so the questions become: In your life, who has helped you see the best in yourself? Who has encouraged you to see yourself as the image of God? And, to whom can you return the favor?

I am grateful to this saint who reminded me of my wings, my ability to fly even as the odds weighed me down. I am grateful that she empowered me to pay it forward.

John 16:33 (*The Message*)

I've told you all this so that trusting me, you will
be unshakable and assured, deeply at peace. In
this godless world you will continue to experience
difficulties. But take heart! I've conquered the world.

Burning Candles

I have read a lovely book of meditations by Father Gregory, a member of the Order of Julian of Norwich. The book is entitled *Words for Silence: A Year of Contemplative Meditations*. Father Gregory is an Episcopal monk living in Wisconsin. The meditations follow the liturgical church year. As I was reading, a particular paragraph caught my attention:

> When one person in a family, in a parish, in a workplace begins to practice being really alive and present in the present moment, not trapped in distractions in her head or lost in his heart, that person is like a burning candle carried into a dark room. People in that person's family or workplace had been sitting in the dark, without even realizing it, thinking that darkness was as bright as things could get. But now, because of the beaming brightness of that person's recollected and whole presence, they are able to see and know deep within themselves just how much more there can be to their religion or their faith. But still, it is only one candle, and the room is still dark. When the flame is passed from person to person until there are many candles burning, then we can really see!"

What a beautiful thought! There have been many times in my life when I have experienced the presence of another as a burning candle. To be in the presence of someone who is so fully present to you, so completely attentive that you feel as if there is no other place that other person would like to be is a gift. In the harried ways we live much of the time, it is a rare gift. Yet it does happen. These are moments, I believe, of true grace.

I would love to say that I have the ability to be so in the moment, so present that I, too, can be a burning candle for another. But, somehow, the distracted life often overtakes me, and I don't even send a spark in the direction of those I meet. It is a practice to improve upon, and what better time than the season of Advent? These dark days call to us to be introspective, to slow down and be in the moment where we have been planted. As we wait and watch for the coming of Christmas, what better desire can we have than to be a burning candle?

The visual image of burning candles reminds me of the tradition of lighting of candles on Christmas Eve. It has been my privilege for many years to be at the front of our darkened sanctuary as the light is passed from one person to another, back each row, until the entire church is lit with burning candles. These candles light the faces of friends, families, strangers . . . all beautiful in the golden glow of candlelight. Some faces are smiling, others show the pathway of tears on their cheeks. Some look far into the distance, offering faces full of memories, while others look out at the beauty that has evolved around them. All faces register wonder.

As we prepare to celebrate the Light of the World, Advent is a time to register our wonder as we are witness to the burning candles among us. It is also a time to be so present to another that we glow.

Button

*Life can only be understood looking backward. It must be lived
forward.*
   —F. Scott Fitzgerald, in *The Curious Care of Benjamin Button*

A button is not something we think about much these days. Buttons are utilitarian, a must. We lose them. We find them. We sew them
back on, and away we go.

As I watched the movie, *The Curious Case of Benjamin Button*, the
opening credits held a frame with a cascade of buttons of all shapes
and sizes. One by one they fell, until the whole screen was a sea of buttons. The movie was lovely, a touching and troubling story by one of
America's greatest writers. But my memory today is not of Brad Pitt or
the amazing actors who told this unusual story. My memory is of my
grandmother.

My grandmother was poor by the world's standards. Her house
was small, warmed by coal heat as were so many in the area. It had
been added onto once or twice, not by architects who measured and
planned well, but by regular folks who knew how to build to serve a
purpose. I would go to her house for overnights, and we would make
peanut butter fudge and work thousand piece puzzles, snuggled by
the heat of the coal burning stove. She lived most of the life in which I
knew her alone, my grandfather having died when I was very young.
I looked forward to those visits because they often included playing
with the button box.

The button box was kept by her sewing machine. It contained
hundreds of buttons . . . small ones, large ones, mostly ordinary ones.
But nestled in the box were also buttons made of mother-of-pearl, or
rhinestone buttons that looked like diamonds. There were colorful
buttons in the shape of flowers. One of my favorites was a navy and
white little sailboat button for, perhaps, a sailor dress. I would pour the
buttons onto a tray and look at them, like someone panning for gold.
Often I would ask if I could take a certain one home and, being given
permission, would tuck the treasure in my pocket.

Buttons are ordinary things. But my grandmother's button box provided for me a glimpse into the mystery of her life before her face was
loose with wrinkles. As I fingered those rhinestone buttons, I imagined
what she must have worn that carried those shiny ornaments. Where
did she wear a dress covered with sparkly buttons? What was she like
when she was young and wearing these glamorous clothes?

As children, none of us can really know our grandparents or parents as they were known by their peers. We cannot imagine them carefree, or cool, or staying out all night dancing till dawn in the arms of someone we've never met. We can only see them through our relationship with them. Those of us who are parents are reminded daily of this fact.

The button box now lives in our attic. It is one of the only things I asked for after her death. I'm glad I have it, for it holds the ordinary and the extraordinary, the known and the mystery, the plain and the fancy, all a part of my grandmother's life. Just as it is for each of us.

A Reminder

There are some things that can wait. Procrastination has its place . . . most closets can wait to be cleaned out . . . laundry can sit for a few extra days in the hamper while a good book is read. But some things cannot wait. Some things, by their very nature, deserve to move to the very top of your to-do list. I learned a difficult lesson about those things that must be done in a timely way.

Last year as Christmas cards began to arrive, I opened a particularly fat envelope. I saw the return address and knew that it was from friends who live out east—friends, to be honest, that I had not seen in several years. The envelope contained a lovely card with season's greetings from these far-flung friends. It also contained all the Christmas card photographs of our children that our family had sent until our lives got too busy to send cards anymore. I held in my hand a pictorial history of our sons' early years . . . Christmas to Christmas. There they were, these beautiful, sweet young boys from infancy to early elementary school. My husband and I, wisely, were only present in a couple of the photos, leaving the true family stars to shine.

I was on the one hand so touched by the fact that these had been saved and returned to us that I was speechless. On the other hand, with tears springing into my eyes, I knew that they had been sent by someone who had been battling cancer for several years. What could their return mean? How was I to appropriately respond? We weren't sending Christmas cards for yet another year and so there would be no quick note of thanks scribbled inside for the kindness of saving these treasures. After the holidays, I thought, when things slowed down, I would sit down and write a letter, catch up, ask how things were going, and thank our friend for collecting our family memories and holding them safely for us.

But life continued on, and I never sat down to write that thank you. There were probably many reasons deeper than I allowed myself to recognize why I never reached out, why I procrastinated. And so, when a few days before this Christmas we learned that our friend had lost her fight, I felt wretched—not only for the loss of this beautiful woman, but also for my frivolous lack of humanity in seeing her gift for what it was. In some small way she was offering a glimpse of the time . . . the precious time . . . that had passed, that was passing, that cannot be recaptured.

And so today I remind myself that there are some acts that cannot wait. I pray for the wisdom to recognize them when they come into my life and for the good sense to drop whatever I am doing and pay attention to what is really important.

The poet Jane Kenyon once wrote a poem called "Otherwise," in which she listed the daily activities that would someday no longer be her privilege to do:

> *I got out of bed on two strong legs. It might have been otherwise.*
> *I ate cereal, sweet milk, ripe, flawless peach. It might have been*
> *otherwise. I took the dog uphill to the birch wood. All morning I*
> *did the work I love. At noon I lay down with my mate. It might*
> *have been otherwise. We ate dinner together at a table with silver*
> *candlesticks. It might have been otherwise. I slept in a bed in a*
> *room with paintings on the walls and planned another day just*
> *like this day. But one day, I know, it will be otherwise.*

Procastination has its place. But we must always be reminded that someday, it will indeed be otherwise.

Kneeling

You are here to kneel
Where prayer has been valid. And prayer is more
Than an order of words, the conscious occupation
Of the praying mind, or the sound of the voice praying.

—T. S. Eliot

I did not grow up in a faith tradition that regularly would kneel to pray. I have vague memories of kneeling at my bedside as a child . . . "Now I lay me down to sleep, I pray the Lord my soul to keep." Frankly that prayer frightened me a bit. My soul seemed too precious, too much a part of me to give away. But my skinny little knees bored into the floorboards of my bedroom as I repeated this prayer I had been taught, looking, I imagine, like a Norman Rockwell painting with my pigtails and flowered pajamas.

Because I didn't grow up as a kneeler, I am always fascinated by traditions where this practice is natural, expected, sometimes even cavalier. I have attended many a mass where I, firmly planted in my pew, watched as those kneeling scratched their heads, looked up at the ceiling, turned to look at who was coming down the aisle. The somewhat flippant kneeling seemed wrong to me. I am reminded of those pilgrims who visit holy places or walk labyrinths in sacred sites, who fall to their knees and walk the last few steps to their destination in this position. Their arrival on bended knee is a mark of their humility, their penance, their praise.

Much of life, I believe, calls for kneeling. The poet Mary Oliver, writes:

> I don't know exactly what a prayer is. I do know how to
> pay attention, how to fall down into the grass, how to kneel
> down in the grass.

As I look back over the last week, there are many moments where kneeling was called for . . . the amazing brilliant red-orange of the hibiscus blooming in our house, thumbing its petals at the frigid temperatures . . . the sunrise I am watching right this minute coming up over the lake . . . the baby whose face I touched on Sunday, peach-fuzz and bright, welcoming eyes . . . the sound of my son's music making, a gift he does not fully realize is his . . . the stories of those who have traveled far and near to walk daily with God. So many opportunities to kneel, it is a wonder that I can stay upright!

Today, this very day, where might you kneel to offer honor, praise, gratitude, awe?

Reflection

Didn't you love the things that they stood for? Didn't they try to find some good for you and me?   —Dion

I grew up fed on the idealism of Martin Luther King Jr., Robert Kennedy, John Kennedy, and the songwriters of the 1960s. At a time when my view of the world was most malleable, these were the voices that inspired me. The words of these people—full of what a more peaceful, unified world might look like—were planted deep in the rich soil of my evolving adulthood. Because I was also an odd adolescent, in love with the church, I interpreted the messages of these leaders in light of my faith, my understanding of this illusive community of God. Some of this happened consciously, but most of it happened without my even knowing. I dreamed, along with Dr. King, of a world in which race would not be divisive issue, where all people would work together for a time of peace. From my faith perspective, this was in line with what I understood to be the call of God in each of our lives.

Waking up this morning I found myself thinking about that young girl—wide eyes, open heart, ready to take giant steps in the world. I am not sure I ever thought about a day when the country I call home, the country I love, would take the steps to elect a person of color to the highest office in our land. As I watched the images of celebrations across the country at President Obama's inauguration— young, fresh, faces full of their future—I felt once again that sense of hope and possibility, the belief in being able to change the world, perhaps being able to realize a time when the things that divide us will become immaterial in the pursuit of the common good.

I thought especially of my high school friend, Marlene Cofer. Marlene was a tall, lanky, light-skinned African-American who loved language. She moved through a room with grace and class, quietly being a grounded presence there. I will not make any claims that we were best friends. That was not a real possibility in a small town in southern Ohio during my teen years. It just wasn't done. But we shared a love of reading, of poetry. When I was with her, I had the sense that I was a part of something fuller than when I was with only my white friends. At a high school reunion a few years ago Marlene arrived carrying a thick anthology of poetry in which her work had been included. There were no other published authors in our class. I was so proud of her for being persistent, for continuing to pursue what she loved while working as a bank teller.

Not long after that reunion, I learned that Marlene had died of a rare and fast-moving cancer. Her beautiful voice, her graceful presence had been silenced, but not before it was preserved in the black and white that writers chase their whole lives.

In Marlene's presence I knew a fuller picture of what it means to be the whole people of God. In my adult years I have known that experience many more times, I am happy to say. And now, perhaps, as a country we might also open our eyes and our hearts to what it means to be the fullness of the American people.

It seems the seeds those powerful voices planted in my adolescent soul continue to find ways to be reborn.

Twice Blessed

On a frigid morning, it would be so easy to write about the cold . . . but I won't. The deep freeze of Minnesota winders has been holding us all captive.

Instead I will tell you about the blessings of my visit to the Como Park Conservatory: What a needed break of humidity and color in frigid days! I highly recommend it. The minute you walk in you are assaulted by moisture, your skin remembers and thanks you by instantly feeling softer, younger. The colors of the spring flowers . . . yellow, hot and pale pink, lavender, peach . . . and the scent of the lilies provide a reminder of things to come.

Walking in the room with fig trees and orchids, I immediately saw a starfruit hanging gingerly near the top of a tree. The orchids were stunning, some fragile and gentle, others bold and bright in their color, their intricate form. Looking at them, I marveled at their existence. How could such a beautiful and amazing sight exist in a world that often seems cold and unwelcoming? For me, it is the certainty of a Source much greater than my imagination that brings such beauty into the world. I experienced the blessing of these blooms, which were tagged to show their once-a-year blooming—and in January or February no less! What a blessing!

But as I stood gazing up at a huge tree, its form reaching to the very top of the conservatory ceiling, a man I'd noticed earlier came near. I had observed him sitting among the ferns, wearing a black robe, reading the Koran. His peaceful countenance drew my attention. Children were flying by, others spoke loudly around him, but he remained calm, centered, prayerful. Now, as I stood looking skyward, he stopped and asked if he might pass by me. I was for some reason stunned by this act of simple graciousness. As I said yes, he proceeded to look straight into my eyes and say, "God bless you." Humbly, I returned the words.

In the cold of winter, blessings still come to us . . . in the beauty of a flower, the scent of summers to come, the healing humidity, and the gentle blessing of a stranger, offering a connection with the Divine.

> *What actions are most excellent? To gladden the heart of a human being. To feed the hungry. To help the afflicted. To lighten the sorrow of the sorrowful. To remove the wrongs of the injured. That person is the most beloved of God who does most good to God's creatures.*
> —The Prophet Muhammed

Liver

Many people have read the book *Eat, Pray, Love* by Elizabeth Gilbert. Being on the *New York Times* bestseller list and an Oprah pick has created quite a readership for this memoir of one woman's spiritual quest. It is a great account of her pilgrimage through Italy, India, and Indonesia as she searches for ways to make sense of the tragedies and insights of her life while moving into her future with hope.

Memoir is a fascinating genre of literature. It presupposes that any given life is interesting enough and instructive enough that other people will want to read about it. The truth is that each of our lives is worthy of memoir . . . the writing down of our experiences, our relationships, our search for meaning . . . but most of us never think to do so. Ms. Gilbert, already a journalist, simply took the time and effort to write her story, probably funded by a nice advance. And her story has touched the imaginations of many readers and helped them see their own life path in new ways, incorporating the wisdom inherent in Eastern culture.

Of all the things I found entertaining and interesting in the book, the words spoken to her by her funky little Yoda-like teacher in Bali keep coming back to me:

> You make serious face like this, you scare away good energy. To meditate, only you must smile. Smile with face, smile with mind, and good energy will come to you and clean away dirty energy. Even smile in your liver. Not to hurry, not to try too hard. Too serious, you make you sick. You can calling the good energy with a smile.

It should be noted that Elizabeth's gift to her teacher, in exchange for his wisdom, was teaching him to speak English. Clearly, some of the syntax was yet to be understood!

But these are powerful words: Smile in your liver, that organ that cleans out all the toxins and junk that gets pulled in through a variety of entry points. Over the last few weeks I have been trying to smile in my liver. In a meeting that seems to be dragging or creating lots of negative thoughts, I focus on an internal smile. When I am stuck in traffic and will be late to wherever I'm headed, I let the muscles in my face relax and allow my inner self to smile all the way down to the gas pedal. When confronted by a rude or angry person, I breathe deeply and give attention to my inner smiling practice. Right now I am smiling. Are you?

To Westerners this concept may seem, as one of my colleagues always says, "Just plain goofy". But I believe there is a deep wisdom in this practice. Another wisdom teacher, Jesus, told the people of his time: "Do not worry about your life. Look at the birds of the air. Consider the lilies of the field. Have faith."

Life is, of course, filled with serious business. But it seems to me the gift of this smiling practice is that it allows us to be open to all the possibilities for creative solutions, for being open to how the Spirit is moving among all the moments of each day.

"Too serious, you make you sick." Wise words. Right now I am smiling in my liver. It feels good.

Psalm 138

I will praise you, O God, with all my heart;

  before the gods I will sing your praise.

I will bow down toward your holy temple

  and will praise your name

  for your love and your faithfulness,

 for you have exalted above all things

  your name and your word.

When I called, you answered me;

  you made me bold and stout-hearted.

Shhhh . . .

God said to Elijah,"Go out and stand on the mountain, for the Holy One is about to pass by." Now there was a great wind, so strong that it was splitting mountains and breaking rocks in pieces before God, but God was not in the wind; and after the wind an earthquake, but God was not in the earthquake; and after the earthquake a fire, but God was not in the fire; and after the fire a sound of sheer silence.   —1 Kings 19:11-12

Sheer silence. When was the last time you experienced sheer silence. It is rare in our culture. We surround ourselves all the time with voices, real or technical . . . music, chatter, news, even when we are not truly listening. The sounds, I believe, do more than fill the air. They help us to believe we are not alone. Some people keep the television or radio on 24/7 as background noise, a virtual soundtrack for the ordinary tasks of their day. Even in church, we fill the worship hour with as much as we can pack in . . . words, music, more words. If we pray too long in silence, people get fidgety.

Last year I took a three-month renewal leave. During that time I spent quite a bit of time in silence, sometimes intentional, other times it was just the nature of what I was doing and the fact that no other human being was around. As an extrovert, it could have been challenging. But what I found was that in the silence, after a period of time, my "monkey chatter" turned off. My mind stopped jumping ahead to "What next?" and stayed in the present moment. The silence became a Presence. Like Elijah I learned that the Holy One was in the silence.

Mother Teresa said, "God is the friend of silence." We see and experience things differently in silence. Instead of being poised on the end of my chair to respond to something someone has said, already preparing my exposition before I have finished listening to the words of the other, to sit in silence and listen, really listen, is a powerful practice. To walk around the lake without words . . . to drive home without the background of radio . . . brings a different perception to the ways we move in the world. The silence can invite us to live in a deeper way.

I invite you to find a time, no matter how small, to be in silence. We are *not* alone . . . the Presence of the One who lives and breathes in all things waits with us in the quiet places. Shhhh. . . .

Attraction

In the early Church people were attracted to it not so much by the preaching, but by the fact that they saw Christians as a community, living a new life as if what God had done was important, and had made a difference. They saw a community of those who, whether poor or rich, male or female, free or slave, young or old, all quite unbelievably loved and cared for each other. It was the lifestyle of the Christians that was witnessing. —Desmond Tutu

After Easter Sunday, the church heads straight into the book of Acts. There is a kind of non-linear path to this from an historical standpoint. The scripture we will read over the following few Sundays has us reading texts that seem to have happened after Pentecost, the "birth of the church," which we celebrate fifty days later. But while reading these stories of the early followers is good for us, good for the church, so little has changed over these two millennia. We are still trying to figure it all out, trying to come up with the right words, the best slogan, the slickest marketing tool, to bring people into the Way. Reading the stories of those first century Christians makes us feel not so alone, not so incompetent.

It is not news that mainline faith traditions have been declining for years. The reasons for this are numerous, and book after book has been filled with, not only the reasons, but also the solutions for what to do about it. In this exploration, it is so easy to go to the fear place and try to do everything possible to "fix" these fragile communities of equally fragile people, hoping beyond hope that we will attract others who want to join us. Most faith communities have buildings that need constant care, constant sources of revenue to keep them chugging along. And in these troubled economic times, at times it can seem futile.

Reading these wise words of Desmond Tutu, I was reminded of what it means to be the church. His idea is that people were attracted to the early church because people "unbelievably loved and cared for each other." How simple . . . how difficult! It is not about the most eloquent preaching, though that helps. It is not about the most beautiful building, though that is awe-inspiring. It is not about the most gifted choir, though that is a treasure. It is not about the slickest ad campaign, though that can generate great enthusiasm. It is not even about the most profound theology.

What attracted people to the Way of Jesus was a community where they were loved and cared for . . . *unbelievably*. And isn't that what we all search for? A community of people who, in the words of Bridget Jones, in the film *Bridget Jones' Diary*, "love me just the way I am." We long for a community where, with all our faults, our failures, our quirks, our idiosyncrasies, we are welcomed for who we are without judgment or question.

In the church, we may not always agree with one another. We may not like the hymns that were chosen this past week. The preacher may have said a few things that really didn't jibe with the way we think. But for the church to be the church, the love for one another must be visible, palpable. Like those in Acts, it is our witness to the world. "I give you a new commandment, that you love one another" (John 13:34).

Bright Ideas

My horoscope read:

> You can come up with bright ideas on your own, but bounc-
> ing off of another luminous mind produces the truly brilliant
> ones. Get together with the smartest person you know to
> start the ball rolling.

I so loved these words that I clipped them out of the paper and have
carried them with me ever since. That morning I was meeting with one
of the smartest people I know, and I shared this little directive with him.
We agreed we were up for what ever work our meeting required of us.

Today I shared this horoscope with my co-workers at our weekly
staff meeting. I told them I had adopted it as my daily horoscope, at
least for the time being, and I implied that I looked to them as luminous minds I could count on. For me these words provide advice to
get up with every day. I can most certainly come up with some fairly
bright ideas, but the truly brilliant ones are those that rise to the top
of a boiling pot of a multiplicity of ideas born out of gathering around
tables, dreaming, discussing, asking questions, a little argument here
or there, a prayer or two . . . and probably lots of coffee. Those are the
places where brilliance is born.

When the apostle Paul described the community of believers as
being like a body where every part was important, I think this is the concept he may have had in mind. Each of us, equipped with unique gifts,
bring to any situation, any community, the raw potential needed to solve
any problem, realize any dream. So many times, we sit by and let others
design the show, and we don't offer what we have beating in our heart.
Or other times, we are so filled with our own bright idea agenda that we
railroad our way past the luminous beings heating the seat next to us.

I'd be happy to share my horoscope with you. As a Gemini, I can
generally say we like to share. So if you are about to embark on a new
adventure, a new life plan, or you just need to figure out what to have for
dinner, I'd suggest phoning a friend for a bright idea. Together your luminous minds might attain brilliance. I'm pretty sure that's how it works.

> *The way God designed our bodies is a model for understanding our
> lives together as a church: every part dependent on every other part,
> the parts we mention and the parts we don't, the parts we see and
> the parts we don't. If one part hurts, every other part is involved in
> the hurt, and in the healing. If one part flourishes, every other part
> enter into the exuberance.* —1 Corinthians 12, *The Message*

Again and Again

I love people who harness themselves, an ox to a heavy cart,
Who pull like water buffalo, with massive patience,
Who strain in the mud and the muck to move things forward,
Who do what has to be done again and again.
—Marge Percy, *To Be of Use*

Do you know people like the ones Marge Percy describes? I certainly do. Our world is full of them. They don't often get the recognition they deserve . . . many times they actually shy away from that recognition. My church is full of them. There are people who spend countless hours preparing, cleaning up, studying, praying, serving, washing hands that are hurt, feeding stomachs that are hungry . . . pulling like water buffalo day after day, week after week.

It takes much patience to do the work of change these days. Massive patience. I see it all around me . . . in schools, in churches, in communities, in our country, in the world. As humans we mostly would like it if things stayed predictable, easy, the "way they've always been." But the truth is the world is always changing, the ways we are called to live and be with one another are always growing and taking on a new shape. Our response to this movement can be openness and possibility, or gritting our teeth and digging in our heels. Both carry with them a degree of pain. But only one will create forward motion, only one will bring about growth.

As I read the scriptures, the evolving story of God in the world is one of forward motion. We are, I believe, moving toward something. It may not be a literal place. It may be, instead, a state of being. Throughout the Hebrew scriptures the people are often on a journey, a pilgrimage, in which each step brings about a greater understanding of how the Holy is revealed. As Jesus walked from town to town healing and bringing hope to those he met, he was followed by people who wanted to become a part of the Way. The Way he offered was a way of change in a world that reeked of oppression and injustice. And so he walked, patiently straining to move things forward.

This day I give thanks for all the saints who have labored, who have given their lives to do what needed to be done. Today I give thanks for all the saints who *are* laboring, who continue to give their lives to what needs to be done . . . again and again and again.

I am about to do a new thing; now it springs forth, do you not
perceive it? —Isaiah 43:19

Soul Friend

Listen to your life. All moments are key moments.
—Frederick Buechner

Once a month, I go into a quiet, beautiful little room with another person. We sit in soft, comfortable chairs. She lights a candle, and we sit in silence for some time. She welcomes the Holy One into our midst, and she prays a short prayer. Then I begin to tell her what has been happening in my life since we last met. She listens. She listens not to try to help me fix some psychological or emotional problem, but to help me hear how the Sacred has been at work in my life. She asks a question here and there. She makes an observation. She might quote Scripture or another sacred text. We end our time in prayer. I leave, sometimes with as many or more questions as I when I arrived, and other times feeling as if I've had the weight of the world lifted off my shoulders. It is holy time.

Today we call such a relationship spiritual direction. The ancient Celts called this relationship *annam cara* or "soul friend." It is a great gift to have someone listen to your life. This soul friend relationship is different than a partner or spouse, even another friend. Those people hear us with a different kind of love, a different kind of listening based on shared history, shared life experiences. A spiritual director is someone trained to listen deeply for how God is moving in the life of another. More importantly they are trained to help the *speaker* really hear how God is moving in their life.

In our fast-paced, deadline-based world it is so easy to keep moving, only hearing the swoosh of traffic, the background banter of the radio, the flip and flop of feet rushing by. Our monkey chatter brains keep us moving from idea to idea, thought to thought, fear to fear, anxiety to anxiety. It is easy to believe that God is not in it with us.

Each month my soul friend helps me stop, look, and listen to the pulls, pushes, and gentle nudges of the Divine. She helps keep me honest in how I choose to live faithfully. She often prays that God will meet me "at my workbench." I always grin inwardly at that image. It makes my work seem much more physical than it is, much more earthy.

For all who are sitting at their workbench, whatever your work may be, may the Holy One sit beside you and bring you peace.

Stunned

A friend spoke to our worshiping community about his own spiritual journey, the twists and turns it has taken, his rebellion, his longings, the push and pull of the institutional church in his life. I am always struck at the courage a person must have to stand before both those you know well and those who are strangers, and talk about some of the most intimate and important parts of life. In speaking he told the story of being in a class in Berkeley, California, with some of the great thinkers in theology, spirituality, and cosmology. It was the beginning days of the class, and information about how the universe works, the sacred nature of it all, was flying through the air. He was, no doubt, taking notes as quickly as he could, feeling a bit overwhelmed with the level of scientific jargon and concepts. At one point, being a good student, possibly anticipating future exams, he asked: "How much of this information are you expecting us to take in and remember?"

The professor answered simply, "Just to the point where you are stunned."

It seems to me that some of the most important work humans do is to be stunned. As I sit looking out my office window an amazing oak tree is rising out of a playground hedged in by massive buildings, asphalt, and concrete; yet it spreads its branches and shades the children who play there, sending oxygen into the air that fills their tiny lungs. Stunning!

There are so many things to be stunned about, and I don't even have to get to scientific language: Tiny seeds that grow into food that fuels my body. Hummingbird wings. A baby's eyelashes. The sunrise that has the full colors of the rainbow and then some. Watching young adult children at the lip of adventure and feeling your heart grow with the promise of their lives. Standing at the graveside of a ninety-four year old whose children were so shaped by her faith and love that they glow with the celebration of her life in the midst of their grief. Sitting beside a young one sounding out words as reading becomes a new skill. The eyes and voices of people singing with joy the songs they love. All stunning!

Perhaps one of the reasons we go for the mundane, that we allow ourselves to be swept away by the unimportant nit-picky details of daily living, is that being stunned can be exhausting. But, oh, who would want to miss the thrill of the Northern Lights or the tart yet sweet taste of a fresh-picked blueberry? Who would trade a meteor shower for cleaning out the garage? Who would choose organizing your sock drawer over staring at the clear, glassy surface of a summer lake?

Think about it. Are you having enough stunned moments in your life? The world is waiting for each of us . . . and there are no exams to be passed. We need only stand with our mouths . . . and our hands . . . and our hearts . . . wide open and ready.

Funerals

I have attended several funerals recently. As a child I went to lots of funerals. In a small town, when someone dies the whole town turns out to pay their respects. It is simply what you do. Now that I have occasion to be in leadership at funerals, it is a very different experience. But always a holy one. I am always blessed to hear the stories of family members and to learn new things, sometimes surprising things, about the one who has passed on. I am always interested in the hymns, scripture, or poetry the person held dear and how the family reflects on those as they talk of their loved one.

Today I attended a funeral of one our dear saints of the church. She had requested a Mary Oliver poem be read at her funeral. It's title is "When Death Comes." The words are beautiful and evocative. They were, of course, meant to express her own thoughts, beliefs, questions—those she had carried throughout her life. But they also, I think, became a sort of reminder or challenge to those in attendance. And knowing this person as I did, I think that could have been her intention. We read:

> When it's over, I want to say: all my life
> I was a bride married to amazement.
> I was the bridegroom, taking the world in my arms.
> When it's over, I don't want to wonder
> if I have made of my life something particular, and real.
> I don't want to end up simply having visited this world.

Even in the sadness I felt at this funeral, I also felt the gentle nudging of this dear, gracious woman. A teacher to the end, she provided for each of us, if we chose to take on the task, an assignment of becoming one who is married to amazement, making something real and particular of our lives. Just visiting is not what it is about. Living is the core curriculum.Really living.

So as I left the service it seemed the sky was a little bluer than it had been earlier, the oak tree outside the church entrance looked particularly lush in the early afternoon light. People's faces seemed vibrant with the flush of summer. And the grapes I ate for lunch were as sweet as could be imagined. Tonight I plan to walk outside and take in the promised full moon, allowing it to bathe me in its light.

I am taking a course in amazement, and I have homework to do. There's a teacher I have known who I hope will be pleased with my work.

Hospitality

All guests who present themselves are to be welcomed as Christ,
for he himself will say: "I was a stranger and you welcomed me."
— The Rule of St. Benedict

I've been involved in many conversations lately that center on the concept of hospitality, of being a host. As a church staff we are exploring the notion of what it means to offer "radical hospitality". . . a hospitality with arms stretched even wider than "welcome," with a heart that offers itself to all . . . no holds barred. It is a fascinating idea to consider: What does hospitality really mean? What does it mean to say we welcome to our home . . . everyone . . . without exception?

This focus however did jog my imagination to times when I have been hosted well. I recall a time after a very cold and rainy camping and canoe trip on the Mississippi River. It would have been an experience I could describe as miserable except for the loving companionship of friends and the beauty of the scenery. At the end of the trip, muddy and somewhat defeated, we dragged our canoes out of the water near a farm that overlooked the Mississippi River. This modest farmhouse, perched high above the mightiest river in our country, was occupied by an older couple. As we hauled ourselves up the hill, the couple invited our soggy foursome into their home. We removed our dirty shoes and were led into their living room where a small table had been positioned to overlook the river. The table was set with plastic lace placemats on which sat bowls of luscious raspberries, freshly picked, swimming in a bowl of rich, white cream. We slowly ate the tart, red gifts of summer. This couple didn't know us. We didn't know them. They simply opened their home and offered what seemed like nectar from the gods. Radical hospitality!

I remember visiting my Aunt Enie at her farm. She was not wealthy in material things, but she had a kitchen table that was always laden with the freshest things from the garden, plenty of coffee and sugary sweet tea. She always an empty chair . . . for whoever stopped by. If she didn't already have a pie or cake resting under white cotton dishtowels, waiting to be sliced, she would go to her freezer and pull out ice box cookies, cut into the roll, and soon the kitchen—no, the whole house—would be filled with the aroma of freshly baked cookies. Radical hospitality!

And then there was my father's funeral. As we gathered, filled with grief and loss, food began to show up at our door. Platters of cold-cuts, loaves of bread, paper plates and cups . . . so we wouldn't have to think about doing dishes . . . even toilet paper. After the funeral, as we gathered in the church basement, this small church of less than a hundred members served everyone lunch . . . two long tables of hearty food and another of just desserts. Each person had offered their specialty, their best dish out of their own kitchen, prepared by loving hands. Radical hospitality!

Hospitality remembered often centers around food. Whether literal food is involved or not, hospitality is an offering of nourishment . . . of being fed . . . of quenching thirst . . . of our best . . . out of our deep knowing that we have enough, more than enough through some perceived grace of the Holy in our midst.

"Then he took the loaves, and when he had given thanks, he distributed them to those who were seated; so also the fish, as much as they wanted. When they were satisfied, he told the disciples, "Gather up the fragments left over, so that nothing may be lost." So they gathered them up, and from the fragments of the five barley loaves, left by those who had eaten, they filled twelve baskets." John 6

Hope Journal

At a party I was surrounded by spirited and intelligent conversation. One woman and I were talking about all kinds of issues and subjects; in the course of the discussion she told me how, after the death of beloved Minnesota Senator Paul Wellstone, she fell into a state of despair. It seemed to her that so much was lost when his plane went down . . . his life, his enthusiasm, his message, her feelings of hope. She then told me about a wonderful task she assigned herself in those days to help her healing begin; she began keeping a "hope journal," writing down those moments of hope she witnessed during the day. I remember sharing her deep grief and sense of loss after Senator Wellstone's death. Everything seemed confused, confusing. So I found this a compelling idea. A hope journal.

It is easy, I believe, to become fixated on the tragedy of our world. Our nightly news and morning papers remind us of all that is wrong with the world. It is rare indeed to see a story of what is *right* with the world. Yet it really is only a small percentage of people who plunder, create havoc, and perpetrate violence. It is a vastly larger percentage of people who quietly and patiently persevere in their simple and humble acts of making the world a better, more beautiful, kinder place in which to live. We are surrounded by them every day . . . sometimes we, ourselves, are those bearers of hope.

I think of the people I know who give countless hours cooking and serving meals to the homeless. They set a beautiful table, invite their friends to provide music for dinner; some give hand massages to those people who have perhaps only known harsh and uncaring touch. I think of the artists who, each day, get out of bed to take up their work of creating beauty and awe-inspiring paintings or sculptures, music to be sung, poems to be shared. I think of the parents and teachers everywhere who patiently teach children to read, to play nicely with others, to develop as kind, compassionate people. I think of the coaches who inspire young athletes to excellence and to develop an understanding of the gifts and limitations of their own bodies. So many, so many people who inspire hope . . . quietly persevering all around us.

Perhaps each of us would benefit from keeping a hope journal. It would help remind us of the goodness that is lived out each day. It would help turn our eyes and our hearts from those situations and people that can bring out the cynic in each of us.

> *The future will not belong to the cynics. The future belongs to those who believe in the beauty of their dreams."* —Paul Wellstone

Snow Globe

You're imaginative these days, so it's hard for you to understand how someone could be without a dream for him for herself. Hold a powerful vision of the future for someone who's lost faith.

I check my horoscope every day. In fact, it is possibly the last thing I read in the paper each morning. After my systematic reading . . . front page, local news, sports, business, finally the variety section . . . my horoscope really represents the words I am most likely to recall during the day as they were the last ones read. Today's wisdom gave me pause.

I checked in with myself. Is it true I am feeling imaginative these days? Well, perhaps not as much as the horoscope would imply, but I am in a stew pot of possibilities, and that is energizing, which breeds creativity. But it is the second part of the daily words that struck home: "Hold a powerful vision of the future for someone who's lost faith." When I read those words, the image that came to me was one of a snow globe in which a scene is held in the shelter of the stagnant liquid until it is shaken to bring it to life with the gently falling snow. Though completely simple in its ingenuity, it is always a thing of magic.

I began to imagine all those people in my life who are experiencing uncertainty . . . friends who have lost jobs, others who are dealing with health issues that cause fear and anxiety, young ones who are struggling to find their own unique way in the world . . . they all represent those who are living on the margins, those who may have "lost faith" in themselves, those they trusted, even in whatever they experience as God—perhaps especially this experience of the Holy One. Each is held in the beauty of that globe waiting for the vision, the light that will help them move into a place of courage, calm, certainty.

Today I can hold out for each of them a vision of safety and wholeness and hope. I can imagine their beauty and the dream that will be reignited or that will flash forth for the first time and will send the snowflakes swirling and dancing, creating that simple magic. Today I can hold for them a vision that their tired or fearful or confused eyes are unable to see. To do this is what it means to be in community, in relationship, a part of the kindom. It is a gift to be the holder and the one who is held. Truth be told, we are always both. Blessed be.

The kin[g]dom of God is not come with things that can be observed; nor will they say, "Look, here it is!" or "There it is!" For, in fact, the kin[g]dom of God is among you. —Luke 17:20-21

Shelter

I find it shelter to speak to you.   —Emily Dickinson

An acquaintance gave me one of the daily calendars with poems, inspirations, and sweet little drawings meant, I believe, to start your day in a positive, lovely way. This Emily Dickinson quote appeared on one of the pages. I routinely miss looking at the calendar for several days in a row, only to read quickly, tear off the day. and use the sheets for scratch paper. When I came upon this quote, I tore it off and tucked it into one of the books I am currently reading.

I have no idea in what context Ms. Dickinson made this statement or to whom. All I know is it is a statement that holds so much . . . trust, intimacy, understanding, reverence, respect, comfort, security, to name a few. What a compliment to have someone say this to you!

Saving the quote has caused me to think of the people in my life who provide shelter when I am with them. I have several friends I can put in that category . . . those who spread their arms wide, listen with pure hearts and open minds, those who don't judge but simply hold my words, my very presence, with love. Certainly many in my family create a shelter when we speak with one another. We listen with ears that have been informed by knowing the subtle nuances only partners, mothers, fathers, siblings, and children recognize after many years of living together.

This image of shelter reminds me of Psalm 91 and the song "On Eagle's Wings" that is based on the words of the psalm. "You who live in the shelter of God, who abide in the shadow of the Holy. You say to God, You are my refuge, the one I trust." The psalm tells of someone who is in danger in countless ways. But when the writer remembers this shelter of the One who surrounds their life, this presence who hears their voice, they are filled with peace and trust that their voice is heard, that they are held in love.

Shelter . . . it is one of the basic needs of humans. Whether built of stone or wood, cloth or mud, we all need shelter. We also need the shelter of those who hear our stories, witness to our lives, listen deeply to our voice. May each of us know this shelter of another. May each of us be this kind of shelter for another.

And God will raise you up on eagle's wings, bear you on the breath of dawn, make you to shine like the sun, and hold you in the palm of God's hand.
                                                        —Michael Joncas

Tattoo

I ran into a friend I hadn't seen for quite some time. He is one of my more gregarious friends, someone you can always count on to be wearing colorful clothes, often things that speak volumes about his values, his creativity. He is a musician, an artist, a teacher, an activist, a composer . . . the list goes on and on. Over his lifetime he has almost always been a part of a faith community. He has led liturgy, written music, and traveled the country helping people express their faith.

One of his first sentences in our conversation was "I don't really go to church anymore. I guess I've lost my faith." It was not really a confession, only a statement of where he is right now on his life's journey. I felt honored that he felt safe to say those words to me. We talked and caught up a bit. In the course of what was turning out to be a very warm morning, he removed the long sleeves of his jacket to expose his arms . . . now filled with tattoos that I'd never seen before. They were brilliant colors—red, yellow, deep blue—and paler shades—a warm brown and rich orange. I asked about these new body decorations. And he began to tell me their story.

He said he wanted to illustrate, in a permanent way, his connection with the four elements . . . earth, wind, water, fire. His left bicep held the earth—a yin-yang symbol swirled where planets often are, stars and water floated all around. This earth sat upon a large grape leaf, and the vines and grapes of the leaf held the earth like a nest. The leaf represented his father, a grape farmer whose fifty-year-old vines now grow in a friend's back yard. His right arm displayed water cascading down, snaking from stream into Celtic knots that moved toward shells that circled his wrist. These shells represented the strong women in his life; the tattoo had replaced a bracelet he had worn in memory of a young niece who had taken her life. He now wears her memory and that of other women who have shaped his journey permanently painted on his right wrist. A fire-breathing dragon encircled his lower left arm. This was a symbol of strength, a connection with the East, one he and his wife agreed represented their marriage and commitment to one another. He was still waiting for the addition of the tattoo that would represent his mother and her influence. He talked for quite some time of all the thought, commitment, creativity that had gone into the palate of his arms.

When he was finished I could only say one thing: "It seems to me you have not lost your faith. You are wearing it." He smiled and nodded his agreement. In his search for a way to express his connection with what he experiences as the Holy, he has chosen to affirm that understanding by painting it with permanence on his arms. While the faith tradition of his youth and early adulthood no longer seems helpful in expressing his faith, he continues to seek to be true to the movement of the Divine in his life.

I am not a tattoo person. I do not like pain. I can barely stand to pluck my eyebrows. But as I listened to my friend express his unconventional faith, his deep connection with the Sacred in his life, I wondered . . . what would my faith tattoos look like? What would yours?

> *All that is of earth returns to earth, and what is from above returns above . . . but good faith will last forever.* —Sirach 40:11-12

Gospel Stories

Two or three things I know for sure, and one of them is that to go on living I have to tell stories, that stories are the one sure way I know to touch the heart and change to world. —Dorothy Allison

Gospel means "good news." We refer to the first four books of the Christian Scripture as the Gospels according to Matthew, Mark, Luke, and John. In these books, their authors, tell of the "good news" of Jesus through their own life experience and world view. Scholars will point out the similarities, differences, and obvious "agenda" of each of these writers. Make no mistake about it . . . these are as much *their* stories as they are the story of Jesus and his followers.

Human beings are innate storytellers. We need look no further than the walls of caves adorned with animals, scenes of battles and conquests, elaborate dances around fires, scenes of sacrifice and honoring, to know it is true. We have stories to tell, and the world needs them . . . especially our "good news" stories.

Each day we can hear, if we want to, the unfolding life story of countless celebrities and their struggles and strife. I am not sure how helpful that really is, to us or to them. But every person has their own experience of those over-reported, always dramatic stories; if in some way good comes from hearing about these famous people, may that good be blessed.

My question is, what about the rest of us not-so-famous people? What about my gospel story, your gospel story? How will the Gospel according to Bob, or Susan, or . . . *you fill in the blank* . . . be told? Whether you write it down in a journal or simply make a mental note of how your story is unfolding, your experience is important. Whether you tell it to a friend or to a stranger, it is a story that needs to be told. Telling our stories, with all their struggles and pain, doubt and questioning, revelation and insight, helps us weave ourselves together as a people, helps us not only remember who made us, but also remember who we are. Telling our Gospel according to . . . touches hearts and has the power to change the world.

Can we hear your story . . . please?

Thank You

If the only prayer you say in your entire life is "Thank You," that would suffice.
   —Meister Eckhart, thirteenth century Christian mystic

One of the first phrases we teach children is "Thank you." Almost immediately after "Mamma" and "Daddy" and "Bye-bye" comes "Thank you." There is a certain sweet simplicity to hear a small child, just learning to speak, utter the words that sometimes only a parent can understand . . . something that sounds like "Thank you." While being given a toy, Cherrio, or cracker, to hear the infant's emerging voice say those words brings pleasure and delight to all around.

Thank you. Simple words, really. We say them all the time . . . to the person who bags our groceries, the gentleperson who holds a door as we struggle with things in our hands, our child who passes the milk in the morning, the neighbor who shares some newly-picked spring flowers. Thank you. Polite words we learned at a very early age.

But "Thank you" as prayer goes deeper. "Thank you" as prayer connects us with the on-going love and care of our Creator, the One to whom all prayers are sent. Thank you for my life . . . for my living . . . for the beauty that surrounds me, for those that stand with me, for the food that is a gift of your earth, for the air, the sun, the moon, the water, oh . . . so many things for which to utter the words, "Thank you."

What is the place of your gratitude today? What gift has appeared in your life that has surprised you and filled you with wonder? How has the Holy One shown up and taken your breath away today?

The syllables are few, the intention deep. Let us pray.

Being Known

People become a part of a community, I believe, for a variety of reasons. People become a part of a faith community for countless reasons. For some it provides a way to express their specific beliefs and to join in with others who do the same. Others join a church because it has been a long standing family tradition. Still others join because they want to engage in ways that make a difference in the world, to tell the gospel story through their actions. There are some who join because they think they "should," and still others who do so because they think others think they should . . . their mother, their wife, their boss, the college to which they might apply someday. I make no criticism or judgment about any of these reasons because I also truly believe that if a person becomes actively engaged in any community, especially a faith community, they will be transformed in significant ways. That is the work of the Spirit.

One of the things a church can offer people is "being known." We exist in a culture where it is quite easy to be invisible if you want to be, to live through whole days where no one calls you by name. I have often said that what the majority of people want when they come into a church community is the same thing Norm received when he walked into the bar at *Cheers*. People want someone to call out their name: "Norm!" . . . to be known, to be visible in an important way to at least one other human being.

I thought of this when our third graders received the gift of their Bible from the church. Being a third-grader is to be in the middle of the pack, so to speak. You do not have the cute factor of being a kindergartner or the cool factor of being a sixth grader, i.e. an "almost teenager." So to be called out from this valley of ages to be recognized, to be known, is a great gift from a community of mostly adults. Many students dressed up for the occasion, families joined them in worship, even grandmas and grandpas if they lived near. Pictures were snapped, and cake was served in their honor. As each student was handed this small black book (with print fit for their young eyes), I saw them look at the gold letters of their name printed on the cover. To have your name imprinted on the cover of a book is impressive at any age.

My sense is that they will forget the cake they ate. They may even forget what they wore. Over the next few years they may even misplace that Bible, though I hope not. I pray they can read those stories and connect it with their own experience of God. Perhaps they will find an answer to a question they have been pondering or comfort for a very trying time. I hope they study its contents and are able to know the story of their faith ancestors. Whatever the case, perhaps in a few years as they clean out their room preparing to head off to college, they may come across that little black book. They may hold it in their now much larger hands and run their finger across the gold letters of their name. Hopefully they will think: "That was a day I was known".

It is one of the things a faith community can offer. And isn't it what we all want?

> *O God, you have searched me and known me. You know when I sit down and when I rise up; you discern my thoughts from far away. You search out my path and my lying down, and are acquainted with all my ways.* —Psalm 139

Psalm 104:31-35

May the glory of God endure forever;

may God rejoice in all that has been created—

The One who looks at the earth, and it trembles,

who touches the mountains, and they smoke.

I will sing to God all my life;

I will sing praise to my God as long as I live.

May my meditation be pleasing to my Creator,

as I rejoice in God.

Story Chair

I receive a quarterly newsletter from a group in Seattle called Earth Ministry. I love looking through it for interesting articles on faith and care of the earth. There are always challenging articles, poems, and prayers written by people who are passionately trying to connect their faith and their daily life. They are trying to create their "life's work" based on how they see the Holy in the world. This is important and challenging work.

My eyes fell on a fall gathering they call Story Chair. It is described as "an intimate, seasonal gathering honoring leaders in the community and inviting them to share how their faith informs and guides their life and their work." Reading the title made me think of the really large, green Adirondack chairs that are placed around the Twin Cities as objects of art in various parks and green spaces. I imagined the story-teller crawling up into the huge chair to tell his or her story, lifted up to the seat of the chair with the help of the rest of the community. The Story Chair would be the focus of the community for that moment, as people listened deeply to the movement of the Holy in the life of this loved one.

At one of our worship services I quoted an article I had read from another magazine. "Every morning we wake up at the intersection of faith and contemporary life, and we offer them Christ." I explained to the community that, while this magazine was written for church pro-fessionals, these words applied to everyone. Each morning we plant our feet on the ground, if we are blessed to do so, and we walk into the culture in which we have been born . . . a culture that for the most part we did not create but are a part of nonetheless. How we take our inner life and mold it with our outer life is the art of being human. This work is not for the faint of heart. There are many obstacles, many things to trip us up, many situations in which we would simply like to turn our backs and pretend that it is another time, another place, a simpler time (or so we imagine) or a time in which someone else is in control, cer-tainly not us. Living faithfully—however we name that—in our time and our world, is the gift and the challenge each of us face. It is the task of integrity and authenticity to which each of us is called.

I wonder how I might tell my story if I found myself sitting in the big, green Story Chair. How would I articulate my faith intersecting with contemporary life these days? How would you? How would you tell your story to the rapt listeners looking up with craned necks and hopeful eyes? The contemporary life we share is complicated. We often think our lives are somehow more complex, more difficult, than those that went before us. I would venture to say that is probably not an accurate assumption. But since it is all we know, it is our only barometer.

I would like to believe that if I sat in the Story Chair I would end my story by quoting the words of Annie Dillard which have always inspired me:"

> *Who shall ascend into the hill of the Lord? Or who shall stand in his holy place? There is no one but us. There is no one to send, nor a clean hand, nor a pure heart on the face of the earth, nor in the earth, but only us, a generation comforting ourselves with the notion that we have come at an awkward time, that our innocent fathers are all dead—as if innocence had ever been. . . . But there is no one but us. There never has been.*

At the end of my story, I hope my friends would lift me gently from the Story Chair. There is, after all, much to be done. And there is no one but us.

Laughter

When God restored the fortunes of Zion, we were like those who dream. Then our mouth was filled with laughter, and our tongue with shouts of joy; then it was said among the nations, "God has done great things for them." God has done great things for us, and we rejoiced. —Psalm 126

How often do you laugh during any given day? How often do you hear the laughter of others? A recent experience of laughter has been my food over the last few days. While nestled in the forest of the Pacific Northwest in what could be considered a truly idyllic setting, I experienced the intoxicating and healing power of laughter. One of my traveling companions has, what I believe to be, one of the most joyous laughs I have ever heard.

One afternoon I found myself outside enjoying a cup of coffee, reading a book in the sun, as I got in touch with my feline nature. Each of our retreat group was off doing "their own thing." Suddenly from what I knew was the front porch of where we were staying, I heard her laugh . . . at first just a loud chuckle and then uncontrollable, body-jarring, roaring laughter. It echoed off the tall pines and the hills around us. I am almost certain it also reached Puget Sound as it continued its rolling sound, drawing me in. I had no idea what the joke was, but I became filled with the joy of the sound. I stopped reading, set down my cup, and allowed myself to be bathed in the sheer beauty of that uncontrolled music until I, too, was laughing.

As I sat there, now removed from my tasks, I imagined the cook in the kitchen halting his knife and slowly turning his head, a smile forming on his face, looking toward the sound of her glorious voice. Tucked in the woods, I thought of the author who was working on a book, stopping at his computer and throwing his head back in a moment of insight and transformation. A mile or so away, children playing on the playground at the nearby school, may have stopped and turned their heads toward the chuckles floating over the trails toward them. They, too, probably broke out into the kind of uncontrolled, body-shaking laughter available, it seems, only to children.

That's what happens with laughter . . . it becomes contagious. I vote we all commit to doing more of it. In a world that is deadly serious, couldn't we all use a daily dose of jaw-dropping, stomach-aching, exhaustion-producing laughter? Who knows what healing and hope it might invoke in the universe?

So Sarah laughed to herself, saying, "After I have grown old, and my husband is old, shall I have pleasure? God said to Abraham, "Why did Sarah laugh? Is anything too wonderful for God? But Sarah denied saying, " I did not laugh"; for she was afraid. God said, "Oh, yes, you did laugh!"   —Genesis 18

Rolling Pin

I never knew my maternal grandmother, Elizabeth. She died in childbirth, giving birth to my Uncle Charles, when my mother was five years old. So it is logical that I have no real memories of her, only those stories passed on by my mother, memories that are filled with the sweetness of a young child's memory of a mother taken from her. Grandma Elizabeth will always be sepia-toned to me, trapped forever in the aging photos I have gleaned from boxes that my mother has saved. Her small frame clothed in the drab colors of the 1920's, she wears an apron over her clothes, her long hair(so I am told) pulled back in a bun at the nape of her neck. She stands in the yard of their home in a hollow near Hitchens, Kentucky, a row house built by the coal mine companies to house the worker's families.

I think of Grandma Elizabeth at this time of year because the one thing I have that belonged to her was her rolling pin. Last night as I was getting ready to bake the Thanksgiving pies, I pulled it from a drawer. It is glass and was meant to have a stopper at one end where you could fill the cylinder with cold water so it wouldn't stick to the dough as you rolled it out. That stopper has long since been lost. Pies aren't baked as often in our house as they were when I was growing up, so the rolling pin only comes out once or twice a year. This probably adds to the visceral experience I have when I begin rolling . . . my hands, my mother's hands, my grandmother's hands . . . who can tell the difference?

As I roll the dough using my mother's recipe, I think of my grandmother's life as it has been passed down to me. She was poor, very poor, but she loved her children passionately and worked to create the best life possible for them. She loved music and taught her children to sing when they were very little. This rolling pin was used to create food to nourish her family, to hopefully provide them with a much-needed treat now and then. As I roll the dough, I am reminded of a poem by Michele Murray called "Poem to My Grandmother in Her Death" :

> Finding myself in the end is finding you
> & if you are lost in the folds of your silence
> then I find only to lose with you those years. . . .
> There's no love so pure it can thrive
> without its incarnations. I would like to know you once again
> over your chipped cups brimming with tea.

Today as I bake pies to be enjoyed by my family, I give thanks for a rolling pin. I give thanks that it is a tangible thing that connects me through time with this woman I never knew, but whose blood courses through my veins. It is a simple, ordinary item, used to make simple, ordinary food. But to me, it is a priceless treasure.

Hebrews 12:1-2

Therefore, since we are surrounded by so great a cloud of witnesses, let us also lay aside every weight and the sin that clings so closely, and let us run with perseverance the race that is set before us, looking to Jesus, the pioneer and perfecter of our faith.

Whirling

Round and round the Earth is turning, turning ever into morning, Round and round the Earth is turning, and from morning into night.

—Chant

On Sunday evening, I was in the presence of whirling dervishes. Really. At the retreat center where I am staying, we were invited to an evening worship experience with a community whose spiritual practice is this form of dance, prayer, poetry, and meditation. Finding its roots in the mystical strains of Islam, it is probably best known to us today as the practice of the poet Rumi. This slowly evolving process leads individuals to an invitation to a whirling dance of prayer and sacred communion with the Holy.

I admit to going out of curiosity. I mean, when have I ever received such an invitation, and when might it happen again? So several of us entered the hall where many were seated on sheepskins and others on chairs in an outer ring. Unsure and a bit self-conscious, we chose the outer ring of seats.

The music was hypnotic and repetitious with a Middle Eastern beauty and simplicity. Those gathered sang a simple two-word phrase over and over, accompanied by gentle hand movements. With each consecutive chant the community moved more and more into dance. First they stood, then they started swaying slowly. Then they began circling in a walking fashion. Finally the entire group moved, without apparent direction, into a fairly traditional circle dance. It was fascinating.

Of course what became the most fascinating was the moment at which certain people would move to the center of the circle and ever so slowly begin to twirl, at first quite deliberately and then with grace and speed . . . spinning, twirling, whirling. One hand gently opened toward the earth while the other reached up toward heaven, they whirled. Eyes closed, they whirled. Around and around, in the same space, never stumbling or bumping one another, they whirled. White robes, blue skirts, flowing outward, they whirled. As they whirled, they seemed almost to not touch the ground, to float instead above it in the smoothest motions I have ever seen.

I have never really watched as anyone entered deeply into prayer. Generally, in our common prayer life, we close our eyes, avoid looking at another, lest we invade one another's private time. We follow along with the words written on the page before us, rotely agreeing to what someone else has chosen for us. It is simply a different prayer life. One might assume we are seeking a different kind of communion with God than those I witnessed on Sunday, but I am not so sure. I can't presume to know what they were experiencing. But I was drawn into the beauty, the warmth, the suspension of time, and held in something powerful by being in their presence. As the music and poetry bathed me with a luminosity that was palpable, I was sure of one thing: We were indeed in the presence of the Holy.

In-Between

After two and a half weeks, I am back on U.S. soil after some time away in Scotland, trying desperately to make a re-entry into "normal" life . . . whatever that is. I have to admit that my mind wanders, and I find myself reliving the sweetness and kindness of the people of Scotland. From beginning to end my experience was one of gentleness, hospitality, welcome, and awe. It seemed each person I met went out of their way to be helpful, to assist me in finding my way. And my experience of the landscape from the lowlands to the highlands to the islands was one of beauty and spectacle that was often too immense to take in. So, while my body is here, for the moment I am living in two worlds.

So it was with laughter that I found myself driving into the office yesterday flanked by two cars: One with a bumper sticker that read "Tree-Hugging Dirt Worshiper." The other read "My boss is a Jewish Carpenter." Of course, the tree-hugger was driving a Prius and the employee of the Carpenter, a Chevrolet truck. I laughed out loud. I laughed because, in some ways, my experience in Scotland, particularly at Iona Abbey, was that the community there embodied both these statements. As a community of people who have worshiped in this place for centuries, they have done so under the banner that they are people of creation, gifted by the beauty and rhythm of the seasons, grounded in the earth beneath their feet. In fact, they say there are two sacred texts: the book of Scripture and the book of creation. They are also deeply grounded in what it means to be people who fashion a life after the example of Jesus, the Carpenter. The liturgy we experienced was rich with images of sun, rain, soil, wind, sea. It was also full of challenges to be people of love, justice and service, prayer and grace.

So many times, at least for me, I have had the sense that somehow the church has told us we had to choose one or the other, soil or Shepherd. And that has always felt false to me, something I could not fully do. On Iona, it was with a sense of "arriving" that I was swept up in the winds and force of the meeting of Prius and Chevrolet. While this theological perspective is one I believe is found in the worship in which I am most often present, somehow knowing that this is the way of naming the movement of the Holy over the centuries in this place filled me with such joy, such a sense of coming home to myself, such an affirmation of faith.

Over the next few days and weeks, I will slowly arrive back here in the place that is truly home. But for now I am in-between. The thread that I hold in my hand, however, connects me to that place where I was reminded that I don't have to choose. It was, indeed, an affirmation that I could have it all: tree, soil, wind, sea . . . Creator, Teacher, Healer, Light of the World. And that the Holy's presence cannot be confined.

> *Now may God who gives seed to the sower and corn to the reaper, give to us all that is needed to produce a good harvest. May God make us fertile in faith, love and goodness, and take us out with joy, and lead us on in peace, as signs of the fruitfulness of heaven. Amen.* —The Iona Community

Tied Together

The reason mountain climbers are tied together is to keep the sane ones from going home.

This anonymous quote is printed on a bookmark sent out by the Minnesota Council of Churches. I read it over several times, discerning its meaning. I knew my heart was drawn to it, but I needed my head to catch up. Since I cannot imagine myself ever mountain climbing, I needed to put it in a context I could understand. It did not take long. It is something I think each of us do most every day. We awaken with the sun and tie ourselves to one another and head out into the world. In our families . . . in our work . . . in our country . . . in the world—we tie ourselves together and pray that when we are frightened or frustrated, when we are weary or wise, when we are joyful and just, we can pull one another along.

Our oldest son who is in college has taken up rock climbing, which I realize is different from mountain climbing. As a parent who is far away from observing this new-found physical challenge (not that I could watch), I do know that it involves harnesses and ropes . . . and climbing with other people. This child who was always at the top of every jungle gym, without a fear of falling, sometimes jumping with confidence to the horror of other adults around, has taken to putting his faith in the safety of ropes and friends to scale rock walls. May God continue to keep him sure of foot and balance.

And isn't that our real prayer as we head out into the challenges of each day . . . that we are held by the invisible ropes of those around us, that we have the strength and courage to hold others, that nothing comes our way that can't be solved collectively with the creativity, sweat, faith, imagination, and commitment of our fellow world travelers? Isn't it our deepest prayer that we need each other so much that we will find a way to solve our differences, share our wisdom, our resources, and our hope? And through it all we pray that God will keep us sure of foot and balance?

There is so much that could and does divide us. But I continue to hold out hope that in the midst of all this, the Spirit will move through our conversations, our arguments, our rhetoric, our fears, and remind us that we are indeed tied together. And in that moment we will tug the rope and give the signal that says, " Go. . . . I'm holding you. . . . Let's climb."

Awe came upon everyone, because many wonders and signs were being done by the apostles. All who believed were together and had all things in common. . . . Day by day, as they spent much time together in the temple, they broke bread at home and ate their food with glad and generous hearts, praising God and having the goodwill of all the people. And day by day God added to their number. —Acts 2:43-47

What Matters

This is all that matters: that we can bow, take a deep bow. Just
that. Just that. —Eido Tai Shimano

Have you taken a deep bow lately? It is not something we do with regularity in our Western culture, certainly not in America. For the most part, we are moving too quickly to bow. And if we all took up this gracious move at the warp speed in which we live, there would be a terrible knocking of heads.

Over the last few days, I have had several experiences that could have used a bow, a deep bow:

One of the dear saints of our church passed on into eternity. We have all known her as someone who was rarely, if ever, without a camera. After her death, a family member delivered two large boxes of pictures chronicling the life of our church—our lives—over the last decade. Each photo was full of faces, joyful faces, caught in the act of celebration. She had a knack for zeroing in on people's faces not only with her camera but with her smiling eyes, savoring and then saving their resplendence. As I looked at image after image, I was humbled by her ability to catch us all at our best. The gift of her keen eye helped remind me of all that is right with the world. I should have bowed deeply out of gratitude.

A young woman I have watched grow up gave birth to her first child this week. I happened to be present when her grandmother came to see this beautiful boy, her first great-grandchild. The anticipation with which this woman approached this tiny one cradled in my arms shone all over her face. As I handed the baby into her arms, I caught a glimpse of the generations connecting in the breath we all shared. What I should have done as I backed away was to have taken a deep bow, honoring the Mystery in which we all stand.

Today I was sitting on my deck, the sun streaming through clouds trying to whip themselves into the frenzy of a summer afternoon rain, when a monarch butterfly made its way from purple cone-flower to orange day lily, swooping, sweeping from flower to flower. Its colorful wings danced in the heat, lighter than air, floating with the grace of a ballerina. I stopped what I was doing and watched, my face slowly emerging into a broad smile. If I had done what I should, I would have untangled myself from my chair and bowed deeply to the beauty of fragile wings.

Each day provides many opportunities for bowing, deep bowing. If we really allowed ourselves, we would begin bending at the waist, allowing our head to dip reverently, embracing what really matters.

Guests

Recently I attended a worship service that had its basis in Celtic spirituality. The music was wonderful . . . bagpipes, harp and drums . . . and the poetry of the words filled me to overflowing. One line in particular from a song has stuck with me: "On the road we live as trav'llers, as pilgrims, as guests of the world." The words were adapted from the words of St. Columbanus, 543-615 A.D., a mystic of the Celtic tradition.

When was the last time you thought of yourself as " a guest of the world"? Isn't it a lovely thought? *"Hello, my name is _____ and I am a guest of the world. "* What would it be like to have that as an introduction? Instead of introducing myself as a wife, mother, minister, woman, sister, whatever, I might say instead, and I would imagine with a certain bit of feeling, " Hello, I am a guest of the world. It is a pleasure to meet you." Perhaps, the words might even call for a deep bow.

Saying those words aloud fills me with such gratitude to this world that has welcomed me. Saying them makes me want to sit up straighter, feel proud of being invited to this celebration, at this time, with all of these beautiful people, with such elaborate surroundings. Think of the differences in our behavior if we thought of ourselves as guests instead of residents or even citizens of the world. I think we might be more inclined to use our best manners, dress ourselves up, walk more gently, and speak more kindly as guests of this amazing planet, this generous earth.

Today is an especially exquisite day. Fall colors are beginning to emerge. The sun is shining brightly. Geese are flying overhead moving from summer home to another. Children are playing with abandon outside. The gardens know that soon the clock will strike, and that their time as guests of this world will be over. And so it is with each of us.

Today, at this moment in time, I pray that you are pleased that you've been issued an invitation to this world, that you have accepted with grace, that you feel as blessed as I do to be " a guest of the world."

Twice Blessed

An early morning walk is a blessing for the whole day.
—Henry David Thoreau

We have a gigantic amaryllis bulb that has been growing in a pot on our kitchen table. Over the last two weeks it has developed five saucer-sized blossoms of delicate pinks and creamy white. None bloomed at the same time. They each had their own coming out day. We, the observers, had to keep a trained eye to the next miracle emerging from our dining table. Over the course of several days, another show of floral beauty dazzled us as we consumed cereal and soup.

Yesterday as I was inwardly lamenting the blossoms that have now withered and fallen off, I noticed what seems like another shoot of green pushing its way up the side of the nearly two-foot stalk that housed these flowers. This morning I saw that it had grown another several inches. I marveled: Could it be possible that yet another shoot would give birth to even more pink and white color? My husband registered his skepticism. It didn't seem probable that we could be blessed twice by one gnarly looking—OK, ugly—bulb. Who knows? But we will continue our breakfast and dinner vigil, watching with untrained yet hopeful eyes.

This waiting and watching got me thinking about the many ways in which we receive unexpected blessings. This morning on my walk to work I was serenaded by a choir of red-winged black birds. These birds, which most often go unnoticed amid their flashier feathered friends, seemed to be singing seduction songs across tree branches. I felt blessed to be present to their love lurings . . . not something I expected on a Monday morning.

A few steps along the same path I passed a man walking his dog. The man was in a hurry. The dog wasn't. His mutt body, weighing in someplace between beagle and corgi, exuded the happiness of walking in a place so full of new life and good scents. As the two humans and one canine crossed the small foot bridge, the dog stopped right in his tracks, looking me square in the eyes. I swear I think he smiled! I know I did as his owner gave a gentle tug on his leash to get him moving. I walked on, having receuved what felt like a dog blessing.

For the longest time humans have tried to relegate blessings to certain places . . . churches for instance . . . but we might as well give in. Blessings are surrounding us all the time. To bless means *"the infusion of something with holiness, divine will, or one's hope."* In the amaryllis plant I see the divine will to give birth, to be beautiful, to save my human self from the grayness of winter days. In the song of the red-winged black birds I heard the hope of summer yet to come. In the eyes of a leashed dog I saw unconditional acceptance and maybe even love.

Twice blessed? Oh, no . . . so many times blessed!

Benediction

Latin: benediction . . . to bless . . . to commend . . . an invocation of divine blessing and the end of a religious service. . . (Webster's New World Dictionary).

The ancient Celts used every opportunity to recall and bless their earthly travels with the knowledge of God's presence among them. From the lighting of the fire that heated their homes to the food they placed upon their tables, from the birthing of a new calf that would someday bring milk for their afternoon tea to the setting of the evening sun, they spoke prayers and blessings on every act that connected them to one another and to the Holy.

It is my prayer that the meditations of these pages have created a new awareness of the ways in which the Sacred shows up in the least expected places, on the many roads we travel in this amazing life. That prayer is held in the hope that the openness of heart offered as gift of the Spirit will be a reminder to notice fellow travelers with a special attention and care so as not to miss the chance to entertain an angel.

And so I offer this benediction in the spirit of the Celtic prayers found in churches, in the illuminated manuscripts for which these ancients wise ones have become known throughout the world, and specifically in the prayers collected by Alexander Carmichael known as *Carmina Gadelica*:

> *The peace of God be with you,*
> *The peace of Christ be with you,*
> *The peace of the Spirit be with you*
> *And with your children,*
> *From the day that we have here today*
> *To the day of the end of your lives,*
> *Until the days of the end of your lives.*
> *The grace of God be with you,*
> *The grace of Christ be with you,*
> *The grace of the Spirit be with you*
> *And with your children,*
> *For an hour, for ever, for eternity.*

Blessed be . . .